COUNTRY PIES

Also by Lisa Yockelson

THE EFFICIENT EPICURE

GLORIOUS GIFTS FROM YOUR KITCHEN

COUNTRY PIES

❖❖❖

A SEASONAL SAMPLER

Lisa Yockelson

ILLUSTRATIONS BY WENDY WHEELER

Harper & Row, Publishers, New York
Grand Rapids, Philadelphia, St. Louis, San Francisco
London, Singapore, Sydney, Tokyo, Toronto

Designer: Lydia Link

Copy editor: Bonnie Tandy Leblang

Indexer: Maro Riofrancos

Library of Congress Cataloging-in-Publication Data

Yockelson, Lisa.
    Country pies.

    Includes index.
    1. Pies. I. Title.
TX773.Y63   1988   641.8′652   87-46184
ISBN 0-06-015915-4

    90 91 92 RRD 10 9 8 7 6 5 4

to the memory of
Lilly Yockelson

Contents

———◆◆◆———

Acknowledgments 11

THE CHARM OF COUNTRY PIES 13

ABOUT BAKING COUNTRY PIES 17

SUMMER COUNTRY PIES 35

AUTUMN COUNTRY PIES 59

WINTER COUNTRY PIES 89

SPRING COUNTRY PIES 109

SWEET AND CREAMY PIE COMPANIONS 127

THE COUNTRY PIE SWAP 132

Country Pies That Use Fresh Fruits and Vegetables 134

Country Pies That Use "Goods on Hand" 135

Index 137

Acknowledgments

———————❖❖❖———————

I have always regarded my "pie file" as a sort of cooking diary—it seems to trace my personal cooking history from its roots, in baking. It progresses from the first pie I ever baked (the Double-Crust Apple Pie on page 62 of this volume) to a modern adaptation of my paternal grandmother's famous Coconut-Walnut-Chocolate-Chip "Candy" Pie (page 86).

Years ago, inspired by the baking prowess of my mother and grandmother (whose pies and cakes filled tables at school bake sales and festivals, and crowded the dining room sideboard on weekends and holidays), I began to collect my own pie recipes. Over the years, I have been hooked on pie making—a pie that looks fresh and tastes of pure ingredients pleases me the most. I will always cherish the time my grandmother and mother spent with me in the kitchen, and in many ways the recipes that make up this charming volume reflect their talents as well.

For their unerring good taste, spirit, and skill, I would like to extend thanks to the following people:

To Pat Brown, my editor at Harper & Row, for the generous amount of time and talent she has brought to this book, and for her good advice and enthusiasm regarding the project; and to her assistant, Toni Rachiele, for the helping hands that smoothed the way for deadlines and like circumstances.

To Susan Lescher, my literary agent, for her caring approach to the details and mechanics of book publishing, and for her much valued support of this book.

To Phyllis C. Richman, executive food editor of the *Washington Post,* and her wonderful staff, for expert advice and direction on food journalism in general and recipe writing in particular, and for allowing me the space in which to publish hundreds of recipes over the past few years. Indeed, the idea for this book evolved out of a recipe story for their food pages, entitled "Sweet vs. Tart: The Rich, Old-Fashioned Pies of Winter" (February 2, 1986).

To pastry chef Ann Amernick and food consultant Barbara Witt, colleagues and friends, for their tasty advice on pies and morale-boosting telephone calls while the manuscript for this book was in the works, and to Marge Guarasci, caterer, who worked the overflow of many pie fillings and syrups into recipes for her parties.

To Nancy Pollard, proprietress of La Cuisine, in Alexandria, Virginia, a fine store that houses a select assortment of cookware and bakeware, for her help in the selection of wooden pastry boards, rolling pins, baking tins, and other pie-making paraphernalia with which I have outfitted my kitchen over the years.

To the warm and knowledgeable owners, managers, and staff of Cox Farms in Vienna, Virginia; Reston Farm Market in Reston, Virginia; and Clarendon Health Foods in Arlington, Virginia. They answered a never-ending stream of questions about produce, loaded crates and flats of fruits and vegetables into the backseat of my car, and hand-picked fruits and vegetables for my appearances at cooking schools and on television.

To José Sandoval, for keeping my home organized and my kitchen in meticulous shape before, during, and after the testing of pies.

And to Steven the Bear, for his love of good food, his support, and his ability to work his way through a vast number of pies (even though he doesn't like plum pie).

THE CHARM OF COUNTRY PIES

*F*rom apple streusel to spicy sweet potato to mile-high coconut cream, country pies evoke an informal, simple goodness. They are casual and old-fashioned and oftentimes hearty; because they are made with pure ingredients, the flavor of the pies is clear and vibrant.

Mary Ellisor Emmerling, author of *American Country: A Style and Sourcebook* (Clarkson N. Potter, Publishers, New York, 1980), describes the overall warmth and easygoing charm of country food in this way: "Country foods are simple, wholesome, and fresh. They are foods that are chosen with care, easy to prepare, and eaten with a hearty appetite. At best they are foods acquired close to their source, whether picked from your garden, fished from the sea, or bought at local roadside stands." Country pies, along with the rest of country cooking, are equally unpretentious and satisfying.

Pie-making is one of the specialties of the true American kitchen. The tradition originated from cooks who had to improvise and create and feed large hungry families and make do, relying solely upon the foodstuffs their own land (or a neighbor's) gave forth. Recipes for pies resulted from a blend of ethnic traditions and personal cooking sensibilities, always making full use of what was seasonal and ripe, or was stashed in the pantry.

The pies in this collection are meant to capture that sense of plain good taste and seasonal bounty. The pies are arranged seasonally, to take advantage of the freshest offerings from the market, farmstand, food cooperative, or garden.

A country pie makes an ideal dessert, whether it is a soft, quivery custard pie, a dense chocolate or sparkling lemon pie, a sweet-tart fresh fruit pie, or one of those rich mincemeat pies. A baked pie set out on a cooling rack, accompanied by a pitcher of Vanilla Pouring Custard (page 129), is irresistible.

THE COUNTRY PIE LARDER

Notes on ingredients from a pie-baker's journal

A country pie is made up of many delicious things: simple larder ingredients, known as "goods on hand" (flour, sugar, nuts, extracts, chocolate); dairy staples (milk, butter, eggs, cream, buttermilk); and a range of seasonal fruits and vegetables. Using what's ripe from the tree or bush, or dug up from the ground, when nature produces it makes for some of the best-tasting pies.

I love to bake all kinds of pies, so my small pantry is continually supplied with the basic ingredients for making them. But I have found that even the most casual bakers keep all the basics for pie making in their kitchen pantries.

Once the cupboard shelves are stocked, any of the pies in this book can be put together with ease. In my pantry, I have set aside a few shelves for all my baking needs. One shelf holds bleached all-purpose flour and plain granulated sugar. I keep the sugar (which is pressed free of all lumps before storing) and flour in enormous apothecary jars sealed tightly with their ground-glass lids; I use big jars that hold 10 pounds each. The contents are continually replenished. Dark and light brown sugar are stored in containers with tight-fitting lids.

Every so often, I make a batch or two of flavored granulated sugar. These sugars are scented with vanilla beans or a variety of citrus peel, such as lemon, orange, or tangerine. Vanilla sugar, for example, is a delicious sweetener to use in all fresh fruit pies and in most custard pies, where the taste of vanilla could be heightened. Lemon-flavored sugar adds a special taste to all lemon-based pies, such as the Lemon Pudding Pie (page 121), Lemon Slice Pie (page 119), Lemon Meringue Pie (page 123), or Lemon-Almond Pie (page 122). I store the flavored sugars in jars next to the plain granulated sugar. Other sweeteners (such as liquid brown sugar and deep amber-colored maple syrup) and other flavorings (such as extracts) are arranged on the same shelf.

Different kinds of chocolate—bittersweet, semisweet, unsweetened, plus miniature chocolate chips—are stacked alongside tins of coconut, cans of sweetened condensed milk, tubes of vanilla beans, and small tins of nuts. Larger 5-pound bags of nutmeats are squirreled away in the freezer for longer storage.

In addition to dairy products, I keep bottles of various homemade fruit syrups in the refrigerator. The syrups are made from fresh fruits simmered in a little water until softened; the resulting strained liquid is slowly cooked with sugar to make a translucent, lightly thickened syrup. I love the way just a tablespoon or so of fruit syrup enlivens a pie filling. The syrups are easy to make and look beautiful in slender glass bottles. The method for making a range of syrups is outlined in the beginning of the chapter on summer country pies (page 37). Beyond adding to pie fillings, syrups can also be added to a fruit mousse or ice cream to build up the flavor; a few tablespoons can be stirred into a tall glass of ice-cold seltzer to make a light and fizzy summer thirst-quencher; or a quarter cup of syrup can be whisked into almost any liquid used for poaching fresh fruit. A bottle of syrup also makes a lovely hostess gift to bestow on any friend who likes to bake or enjoys making desserts.

ABOUT BAKING COUNTRY PIES

A country pie is the perfect union of a simple filling and a light, tender pie crust. The filling may be sliced fresh fruit, sweetened, spiced, and lightly bound with cornstarch; a thin egg-and-cream-fortified mixture which bakes into a trembling custard; or a wicked coconut-walnut-chocolate-chip filling, reminiscent of a fudgy candy bar.

The pie crust is plain and buttery—nothing more than butter cut into the flour until reduced to small, crumbly flakes. A blend of egg yolk and ice-cold water binds it into a pliable dough. The pie dough is rolled out with a sturdy rolling pin and fitted into a standard sloping 9- or 10-inch pie tin. The top of a double-crust or deep-dish pie can be festooned with cutouts of pastry dough pressed onto the lid in a whimsical pattern.

The rolling pin I use is a straight 3-inch-thick dowel of smoothly polished oak, without ball-bearing handles. The pin is the same thickness throughout. I collect old-fashioned antique pie tins, the kind with a brand name imprinted on the bottom, such as "Mrs. Smith's Mellow Rich Pie," "Holmes," "Crusty Pie," or "Mrs. Wagner's Pies." A long time ago, when you bought a pie in its baking tin, a 10- or 15-cent deposit was added to the cost of the pie. Now the tins are among the important collectibles of American bakeware. Some of my tins have bottoms with several small holes; the holes let the heat of the oven penetrate the pie shell directly, for an extra-crispy crust.

Pie pans made out of tin help to turn the crust golden brown and flaky; tin also retains the heat so the pie crusts hold their shape. Fluted edges and pastry cutouts applied to the top of a pie baked in a tin pie pan retain their shape, too.

Country pies are usually baked in standard 9- or 10-inch pie tins that are between 1½ and 1¾ inches deep. If a recipe calls for a deep 9-inch pie pan, select one between 2 and 2¼ inches deep. Some old pie tins were made 2 to 2½ inches deep; look for them at flea markets, tag sales, and antique shows. A plain 10-inch pie pan can be substituted for a deep 9-inch tin, with excellent results.

Most of the pie fillings, with the exception of those cooked in a saucepan on the stovetop, can be put together in a large mixing bowl. I like to combine ingredients for a pie filling in a classic "batter" bowl. My batter bowl has the traditional pouring spout and easy-to-grab handle, holds about 10 cups, and is made of glazed pottery. If I am filling a pie shell with a liquid mixture, I just tip my batter bowl over the pastry shell and pour; fruit mixtures get spooned out from the bowl and any juices that linger get poured over the filling.

Once a double-crust or deep-dish pie is assembled, the top crust can be decorated with cutouts of pastry dough. Or you can design a cover of cutouts to apply over the filling of a double-crust pie instead of a solid cover. To make a pattern of cutouts use a cookie cutter to stamp out shapes from a sheet of pie dough. Cookware and hardware stores (and even some supermarkets) offer a large selection of shapes—animals of all kinds, scalloped rounds, hearts, flowers, leaves, stars, and so on. Nests of cutters, such as graduated heart-shaped cookie cutters, are good to have on hand and are fun to work with, as are the tiny cutters designed to stamp out aspic.

———————————❖❖❖———————————

FLAKY PIE CRUSTS

A flaky pie crust is what good pie baking is all about, and whoever said that a pie crust should be made with a warm heart and a cold hand was a very wise person.

Years ago, I perfected two recipes for pie dough, one for a single-crust pie shell and another for a double-crust pie shell. Each dough is lightly sweetened and flaky, and bakes to a handsome golden brown color. A single-crust pie shell made out of Flaky Pie Crust (recipe follows) is strong enough to hold any kind of filling. The Flaky Pie Crust for a Double-Crust Pie (page 30) bakes up tender but sturdy and is perfect for enclosing all kinds of fruit fillings. With these two recipes in hand, you'll be able to make all the pies in this book.

Pie crusts are simple and rewarding to assemble, whether made by hand or in a food processor. Both procedures have been outlined in each of the pie crust recipes. When making pie dough, remember all liquids and fats should be used cold so your pie crust will bake up tender and flaky. When working with pie dough, your hands should be cool; if they are warm, rinse them in cold water before handling the dough.

❖❖❖❖❖❖❖❖❖❖❖❖❖❖❖

Flaky Pie Crust

1½ cups all-purpose
flour (stir gently to
aerate the flour;
measure by scooping
down into the flour
with a dry measure
and level the top with
a straight edge of a
knife)

¼ teaspoon salt

8 tablespoons (¼ pound
or 1 stick) cold
unsalted butter, cut
into tablespoon chunks

1 tablespoon granulated
sugar

1 extra-large egg yolk,
cold

2 tablespoons ice-cold
water, or more as
needed

1 extra-large egg white,
for waterproofing,
optional (page 24)

---

*Makes enough pie dough for
one 9- or 10-inch single-crust
pie or one pastry cover for a
9- or 10-inch deep-dish pie*

This buttery pie dough is the one I've been using for many pie-baking years; it's flaky and tender, yet stands up to any kind of filling, whether fruit-based, custard- or pudding-like, or the thin and rich filling for a translucent pie, such as pecan. The dough is especially easy to patch, holds up beautifully in humid weather, and takes well to pinching and crimping into a fluted edge.

The flaky pie crust can be rolled out and fitted into the pie pan, popped into a self-sealing plastic bag, and refrigerated for up to two days before baking. Unbaked pie crusts freeze well, too (see "To freeze a pie shell," page 25).

To make the dough by hand, stir the flour and salt together in a large mixing bowl. Add butter and, using two round-bladed knives, cut into the flour until reduced to small bits. Using the tips of your fingers, further blend the fat into the flour by dipping down into the mixture and crumbling it between your fingertips as you are lifting it to the surface. The mixture should look like coarse cornmeal. Sprinkle with sugar and stir in with a few brief strokes. Blend together the egg yolk and water in a small mixing bowl. Pour over the flour mixture. Quickly combine to make a firm but pliable dough, using a fork or the fingertips of one hand. (Keep the other hand clean for answering the telephone, which always seems to ring when you are trying to make a pie dough.) Add additional droplets of ice-cold water if the dough seems too dry or crumbly. Turn out the dough onto a large sheet of waxed paper, shape into a rough, flat cake, and wrap with the paper. Refrigerate for 15 to 20 minutes.

To make the dough in a food processor, place the flour and salt in the work bowl of a food processor fitted with the steel knife. Add the butter and process, using quick on-off pulses, until the butter is reduced to small flakes. Sprinkle with the sugar and process for 1 to 2 seconds to blend. Beat the egg yolk and water in a small mixing bowl and pour over the flour-butter mixture. Process, using short, on-off pulses, until the dough begins to mass together. Add extra droplets of water if the dough seems crumbly or dry. Turn out the dough onto a large sheet of waxed paper, shape into a flat cake, and wrap with the paper. Refrigerate the dough for 15 to 20 minutes.

To roll out the pie dough, tear off two long sheets of waxed paper at least 17 to 18 inches long. Place the dough in the center of one sheet of waxed paper and top with the remaining sheet. Gently press the top sheet. Using short, quick, rolling motions, roll the dough to a scant ¼-inch thickness (approximately 13 inches in diameter). Transfer to a cookie sheet and chill for 20 minutes.

To line a rimmed pie pan, peel off the top layer of waxed paper from the sheet of pie crust. Cut strips of dough about ⅓ inch thick from the outside of the circle of dough, keeping the shape intact as you cut away strips of dough. Lightly brush the rim of the pie pan with cold water, press the strips onto the rim, and lightly brush with cold water. Invert the circle of dough onto the bottom of the pan and peel off the waxed paper. Press the dough lightly on the bottom first, then up and against the sides. Press the overhang of dough onto the rim and cut off the overhang using a sharp paring knife. Make long ¹⁄₁₆-inch-deep scoring marks on the outside edges of the dough to "rough up" the rim and give it some texture and thickness. Flute or crimp the edges decoratively, using the sampler of finished edges on page 27 as a guide.

Prick the bottom of the pie shell with the tines of a fork. Refrigerate, loosely covered, for about 30 minutes. For longer storage, wrap in a sheet of plastic, slide into a large plastic bag, and seal, and refrigerate or freeze. Save the dough scraps, bag separately, and refrigerate; use to patch tears in a pie shell.

To cover a deep-dish pie with a round of pie dough, peel off the top layer of waxed paper from the sheet of pie crust. Cut strips of dough about ⅓-inch thick from the outside of the circle of dough. Lightly brush the rim of an ovenproof oval or round deep-dish pie pan with cold water; press on the strips of dough. Spoon the filling into the pie dish, mounding it slightly. Brush the top of the pastry-lined rim with cold water. Lay the pie crust over the filling by inverting the circle of dough over the filled pie pan. Peel away the waxed paper. Press the dough firmly around the rim. Cut away any overhang of dough using a sharp paring knife. Make long ¹⁄₁₆-inch scoring marks on the outside edges of the dough to "rough up" the rim and give it some texture and thickness. Flute or crimp the edges decoratively, using the sampler of finished edges on page 27 as a guide.

If you are using pastry cutouts, place on the top crust by brushing each with cold water and affixing to the crust. Refrigerate for 10 minutes, then glaze and cut several steam vents in the top crust.

To completely prebake a pie shell, line the well-chilled pie shell with a single length of aluminum foil. Fill with raw rice or dried beans. Preheat the oven to 425° with a cookie sheet on the lower-third level rack. Bake the pie on the cookie sheet for 10 minutes, remove the foil and rice, reduce the oven temperature to 375°, and continue baking for 10 to 12 minutes longer, or until baked through and a medium-amber color. Prebaked pie shells are used throughout this book when single-crust pie shells are called for; prebaking the crust guards against soggy or underbaked pie crusts, and vastly improves the taste and texture of the finished pie.

To waterproof the pie shell, remove the shell from the oven a few minutes before it finishes baking. Lightly beat an egg white until frothy. Brush the inside of the pie shell up to the decorative rim with the beaten white, using a soft pastry brush. Return to the oven for 1 to 2 minutes longer to finish baking and to dry the egg wash. The pie shell is now ready to be filled.

I like to waterproof the inside of a single-crust pie to keep the pastry shell from becoming soggy and damp after it is filled.

I always waterproof pie shells when I am making custard pies [Vanilla Custard Pie (page 92) and Coconut Custard

Pie (page 93)], streusel pies [Apple Streusel Pie (page 104), Peach Streusel Pie (page 38), and Cinnamon-Pear Pie with Walnut Streusel (page 69)], lemon pies [Lemon Pudding Pie (page 121), and Lemon-Almond Pie (page 122)], all the vegetable custard pies [Pumpkin Custard Pie (page 76), Pumpkin Crunch Pie (page 78), Orange-Butternut Squash Pie (page 82), Apricot-Yam Pie (page 81), Brandied Golden Acorn Squash Pie (page 84), and Fresh Sugar Pumpkin Pie (page 80)], and for Brown Sugar Pie (page 87), Lime Cream Pie (page 126), and Buttermilk Pie (page 106).

To freeze a pie shell, wrap in several sheets of plastic wrap, slide into a self-locking plastic bag, and freeze. The pie shell should be used within two months; bake directly from the freezer without defrosting.

For a frozen single-crust pie shell, increase baking time at 375° by 5 to 6 minutes, or until the shell is a golden brown color.

VARIATIONS

To vary the basic recipe for Flaky Pie Crust dough, use the following additions or substitutions:

Substitute *¼ cup cold solid shortening* for half of the butter, for a pie crust with a more fragile, melting crumb.

Substitute *½ cup of cold pure rendered lard* for the entire amount of butter, for a tender crust to use for apple or pear pies, and for pies that combine fruit and nuts or fruit and mincemeat.

Blend *½ teaspoon ground cinnamon, ¼ teaspoon freshly grated nutmeg, and ¼ teaspoon ground ginger* into the flour with the salt, for a spicy pie crust that tastes right with all kinds of fruit pies, sweet vegetable custard pies (such as pumpkin, acorn squash, and butternut squash), and fruited mincemeat pies.

Add *¼ teaspoon pure vanilla extract* to the egg yolk and ice-cold water mixture to lightly flavor the crust; this crust is appealing with any kind of fruit, nut, or custard pie.

A SAMPLER OF PIE FINISHES

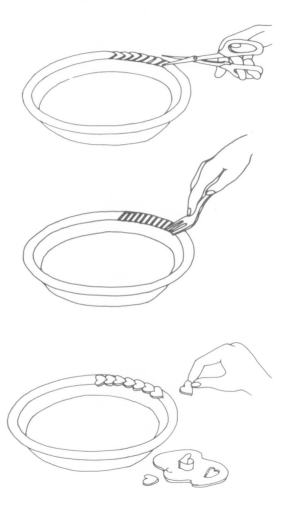

FEATHERY EDGE

With the open tip of a pair of scissors, cut slanting V's around the edge of the pie crust, spacing each cut ½ inch apart.

SIMPLE FORK-FLUTED EDGE

Press the back of the tines of a fork firmly into rim of pie crust, using a quick rocking motion. Repeat around pie crust edge.

HEART-SHAPED EDGE

With a small heart-shaped cutter, stamp out hearts from sheet of pastry dough. Lightly brush rim of crust with cold water; place hearts around rim, overlapping slightly, pressing down gently to adhere.

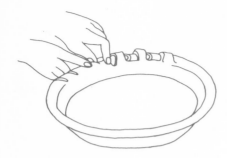

CHECKERBOARD EDGE

Omit long scoring marks designed to give depth to edge of pie crust (page 23). Cut pie crust edge at ½-inch intervals, making each cut ½ inch long, creating square tabs. Roll or fold down every other section.

RUFFLED EDGE

Press left thumb on rim of pie crust. Draw the back of a knife (blunt edge) in toward the center of the pie about ½ inch. Repeat at even intervals around rim of crust, creating deep ruffled scallops.

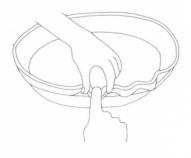

PINCHED SCALLOPED EDGE

Put forefinger of right hand on edge of pie crust. Pinch dough into a deep scallop with forefinger and thumb of left hand by drawing in the dough about ¼ inch. Repeat at even intervals around rim of crust.

LEAFY EDGE

With a sharp paring knife or leaf-shaped cutter, cut small oval-shaped leaves from a sheet of pastry dough. With the back of a knife, mark veins on the leaves. Lightly brush rim of crust with cold water; place leaves touching each other, zigzag fashion, around rim of crust, pressing down gently to adhere.

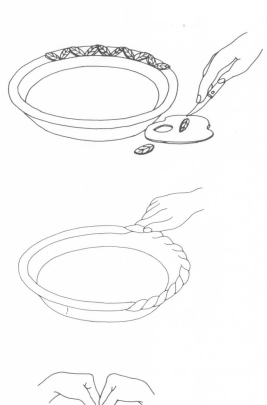

SQUEEZED ROPE EDGE

Press thumb of right hand on edge of pie crust at a slight angle. Squeeze pie dough edge at even ½-inch intervals between thumb and knuckle of forefinger to create a rope effect.

HIGH PEAKED EDGE

Using thumb and forefinger of both hands, pinch together ½-inch sections of pie crust edge, creating a rim that stands up. Repeat at even intervals around edge of crust.

Flaky Pie Crust for a Double-Crust Pie

2 cups all-purpose flour (stir gently before measuring to aerate the flour; measure by scooping down into the flour with a dry measure and level the top with the straight edge of a knife)

¼ teaspoon salt

10⅔ tablespoons (¼ pound or 1 stick plus 2⅔ tablespoons) cold unsalted butter, cut into tablespoon-size chunks

1 tablespoon plus 1 teaspoon granulated sugar

1 extra-large egg yolk, cold

3 tablespoons ice-cold water, or more as needed

This is an ideal pastry dough to use for double-crust pie; it bakes up golden and flaky, and holds its shape.

To make the dough by hand, stir the flour and salt together in a large mixing bowl. Add butter and, using two round-bladed knives, cut into the flour until reduced to small bits. Using the tips of your fingers, further blend the fat into the flour by dipping down into the mixture and crumbling it between your fingertips as you are lifting it to the surface. The mixture should look like coarse cornmeal. Sprinkle with sugar and stir in with a few swift strokes. Blend together the egg yolk and water in a small mixing bowl. Pour over the flour mixture. Quickly combine to make a firm but pliable dough, using a fork or the fingertips of one hand. Add additional droplets of ice-cold water if the dough seems too dry or crumbly. Divide the dough in half and press each half into a flat cake on separate sheets of waxed paper. Wrap dough and refrigerate for 15 to 20 minutes.

To make the dough in a food processor, place the flour and salt in the work bowl of a food processor fitted with the steel knife. Add butter and process, using quick on-off pulses, until the butter is reduced to small flakes. Sprinkle with the sugar and process for 1 to 2 seconds to blend. Beat the egg yolk and water in a small mixing bowl and pour over the flour-butter mixture. Process using short on-off pulses until the dough begins to mass together. Add extra droplets of water if the dough seems crumbly or dry. Divide the dough in half and press each half into a large, flat cake on separate sheets of waxed paper. Wrap the dough and refrigerate for 15 to 20 minutes.

1 extra-large egg white,
  beaten until frothy,
  for waterproofing the
  unbaked pie shell,
  optional

---

*Makes enough pie dough for
one 9- or 10-inch double-
crust pie, or one 9- or 10-
inch cover for a deep-dish
pie with dough left over
to make pastry cutout
decorations for the top
of the pie.*

To roll out the pie dough, tear off four long sheets of waxed paper at least 17 to 18 inches long. Place each cake of dough in the center of one sheet of waxed paper and cover with another sheet, gently pressing each top sheet. Using short, quick rolling motions, roll out the dough to a thickness of a scant ¼ inch; each round of dough will be about 10-11 inches in diameter. Transfer each to a cookie sheet and chill for 20 minutes.

To freeze pie crust dough, wrap the rolled-out dough, on its waxed paper sheets, in several layers of plastic wrap, carefully slide into a self-locking plastic bag, and freeze for up to two months.

To use frozen dough in making a double-crust pie, lift two sheets of dough from the freezer to the refrigerator for about half an hour or until pliable. Remove dough from the refrigerator, peel off the waxed paper, and assemble the pie according to the instructions below.

To line a rimmed pie pan for a double-crust pie, remove one sheet of pastry dough from the refrigerator. Peel off the top layer of waxed paper. Cut strips of dough about ⅓-inch thick from the outside of the circle of dough, keeping the shape intact as you cut away strips of dough. Lightly brush the rim of the pie pan with cold water, press the strips onto the rim, and lightly brush with cold water. Invert the circle of dough onto the bottom of the pan and peel off the waxed paper. Press the dough lightly on the bottom first, then up and against the sides. Press the dough onto the rim and cut off the overhang using a sharp paring knife. If you are making the shell in advance, wrap it in a self-sealing bag and refrigerate. About 15 minutes before filling the shell, beat the egg white until frothy and brush it on the inside of the pastry shell to waterproof it; this is an optional step, but I recommend it highly to keep the bottom crust crisp. Refrigerate for 15 minutes.

Fill the pastry-lined and waterproofed shell with the filling, mounding it slightly toward the center. Lightly brush the pastry rim with cold water. Peel off the top layer of waxed paper from the second circle of dough. Invert the circle of dough over the pie filling. Peel away the sheet of waxed paper. Press the dough firmly onto the moistened rim. Cut away any overhang of dough using a sharp knife. Make long $\frac{1}{16}$-inch scoring marks on the outside edges of the dough to give some texture and thickness to the rim. Flute or crimp the edges decoratively, using the sampler of finished edges on page 27 as a guide.

If you are using pastry cutouts, place on the top crust by brushing each with cold water and affixing to the crust in an attractive pattern. Refrigerate for 10 minutes, then glaze and cut several steam vents in the top crust.

To fashion a pie cover of pastry cutouts, select a cookie cutter for stamping out cutouts. Diamonds, hearts, scalloped rounds, triangles, rectangles, animals, or fruits are all distinctive shapes. Stamp cutouts from the second sheet of dough and chill on a cookie sheet. After the filling has been piled into the pie shell, cover the top with the cutouts, overlapping one over the next to form a top crust. Since some small patches of filling will show through, cutting steam vents in the top crust is not necessary. Chill the pie for 10 minutes, then glaze the cutouts, and bake as directed. A cutout pastry top is a whimsical and unusual touch to finish off a double-crust or deep-dish pie. It works best for deep-dish fruit pies, some pear pies [Pear Mincemeat Pie (page 68) and Spiced Pear-Currant Pie (page 71)], the Apple-Ginger Mincemeat Pie (page 63), Apple-Pear Pie with Apple Cider Syrup (page 66), and the Cranberry-Walnut Mincemeat Pie (page 72).

To make a lattice cover for a double-crust pie, cut long, narrow 1-inch wide strips, wide 1½ to 2-inch wide strips, or extra-wide 2 to 3-inch strips from one round of pie dough using a fluted pastry wheel or a sharp knife and a ruler. Place the strips on a waxed paper-lined cookie sheet and refrigerate for 20 minutes. Line the pie tin with the second round of pie dough according to the directions on page 31, ("To line a rimmed pie pan for a double-crust pie"), to the point of fluting the edges. The edges are left unfluted so that lattice strips can be pressed on later.

Pile the filling into the pie crust. Weave the strips of dough over the filling, securing them by pressing firmly where the rim and lattice strip come together. Trim off any overhanging edges. Flute or crimp the edges decoratively and chill for 10 minutes before baking.

To add extra pastry cutouts to the top of a deep-dish or double-crust pie, you'll need to make one recipe of Flaky Pie Crust (page 21) in addition to one recipe of Flaky Pie Crust for a Double-Crust Pie (page 30). From the extra round of pastry dough, cut out shapes using a cookie cutter or a stencil and a sharp paring knife. A cutout of a cornucopia, for example, would be nice to apply to the top of a double-crust pie served on Thanksgiving; fruit cutouts are a nice touch to add to a double-crust fruit pie. Always cut out shapes from a well-chilled sheet of dough. Brush one side with cold water and press on the top crust. Glaze the pie and bake as directed.

VARIATIONS

To vary the basic recipe for Flaky Pie Crust for a Double-Crust Pie, use the following additions or substitutions:

Substitute *5⅔ tablespoons of cold solid shortening* for part of the butter (thus using a mixture of 5 tablespoons butter and 5⅔ tablespoons solid shortening); use with any double-crust apple, pear, or fruited mincemeat pies, or the double-crust Lemon Slice Pie (page 119).

Substitute *10⅔ tablespoons cold pure rendered lard* for the entire amount of butter; use with any double-crust fresh fruit pies or any double-crust pies with a mincemeat filling.

Blend *½ teaspoon ground cinnamon, ½ teaspoon freshly grated nutmeg, and ½ teaspoon ground cloves* into the flour with the salt, for a spicy pie crust that tastes right with any of the double-crust fresh fruit pies.

Add *½ teaspoon pure vanilla extract* to the egg yolk and ice-cold water mixture; use this lightly flavored dough with any fresh fruit double-crust pies in the summer section.

SUMMER
COUNTRY
PIES

SUMMER COUNTRY PIES

————◆◆◆————

Peach Streusel Pie   38
Deep-Dish Gingered Peach Pie   40
Double-Crust Blueberry-Peach Pie   42
Deep-Dish Blueberry Pie   44
Spiced Red Plum Pie   45
Prune Plum Pie   46
Deep-Dish Walnut-Rum-Plum Pie   46
Double-Crust Nectarine Spice Pie   48
Sour Cherry Pie   50
Glazed Yellow Cherry Pie   51
Deep-Dish Blackberry Pie   52
Apple-Raspberry Pie   53
Red Raspberry Pie   54
Fresh Apricot Pie   55
Late Season Green Tomato Pie   56

*P*ies made in the summertime, loaded with sliced fresh fruit or perfect berries, are a delight. Make several rounds of pie crust dough and stack in the freezer. When you come from the farm market with an armload of ripe fruit, remove a round of dough from the freezer to make a quick-from-scratch pie.

I always buy more fruit than I need for any one pie (or other dessert) and turn the extra into fresh fruit syrups, which I love to use in summer pie fillings. Fruit syrups are made from chunked or sliced ripe fruit, water and granulated sugar. The syrups are clear and lightly thickened—like having the essence of summer in a bottle. I almost always have six—or more—syrups on hand. I find them appealing to use in making fruit compotes, for swirling into ice cream, in mousse mixtures, and as syrup solutions for poaching fruit.

I make fruit syrups from peaches, red plums, blue plums, apricots, blueberries, red raspberries, black raspberries, sweet Bing cherries, sour "pie" cherries, yellow cherries, and nectarines. Whole fruits are sliced or cut into large cubes, with their skins and pits still attached for color and flavor. Cherries are only lightly crushed.

Fresh Fruit Syrups

To make the syrup, place 8 cups of the prepared fruit in a large nonreactive casserole. Such a casserole should be made out of stainless steel, enameled cast iron, or release-surface-coated aluminum; those substances will not taint the contents with a metallic taste. Add 1½ cups of water, cover and simmer until the fruit is tender and falling apart, about 20 minutes. Remove from the heat and let stand, covered, for 5 mintues. By cupfuls, drain the fruit in a large stainless steel sieve set over a big bowl. Press on the solids once or twice to extract the juice, being careful not to mash the pulp through the sieve. Measure the pressed juice.

Pour the juice into a clean casserole and, for every cup of juice, add 1 cup granulated sugar. Cover and cook slowly until the sugar has dissolved. Uncover and simmer the syrup until lightly thickened, about 10 minutes, depending on the density of the fruit used. Cool to room temperature, funnel into clean, dry bottles, cap tightly, and refrigerate.

Two tablespoons of fruit syrup can be added to any filling for a deep-dish pie, and 1 to 2 tablespoons can be spooned over the fruit filling in a double-crust pie.

❖❖❖❖❖❖❖❖❖❖❖❖❖❖❖❖❖

Peach Streusel Pie

¼ cup plus 2 teaspoons all-purpose flour

½ cup granulated sugar

¼ cup light brown sugar, firmly packed

¼ teaspoon ground cinnamon

This homestyle pie has two dimensions: an aromatic layer of peaches thickened with flour and seasoned with sugar, cinnamon and lemon juice, and a crunchy pile of nutty crumbs covering the peaches. The nut-sugar-flour streusel topping makes a perfect covering for almost any kind of juicy summer fruit—it's a lightly crunchy cloak that seals in the fruit as it bakes. The filling for this pie is baked in a fully baked pie shell, which I recommend to keep the pastry dough crisp. Baking the filling in an unbaked shell of dough would produce a partially cooked crust and a quite soggy one at best.

5 cups peeled, pitted, and sliced peaches (about 7 large peaches), tossed in 1 tablespoon freshly squeezed lemon juice

one fully baked 9-inch pie shell, made from one recipe Flaky Pie Crust (page 21)

FOR THE SUGAR AND SPICE STREUSEL:

¾ cup all-purpose flour

½ teaspoon ground cinnamon

¼ teaspoon freshly grated nutmeg

¼ cup granulated sugar

¼ cup light brown sugar, firmly packed

½ cup chopped walnuts

5 tablespoons cold unsalted butter, cut into small chunks

One 9-inch pie

White peaches, if you can get them, make a succulent pie, as do the end-of-summer freestones, with their deep pink blush and sweet flesh.

Serve big slices of this pie with Double Vanilla Ice Cream (page 130) or Vanilla Pouring Custard (page 129). The ice cream will melt into the juice of the pie filling for a delicious mingling of flavors.

——————❖❖❖——————

Blend together the flour, granulated sugar, light brown sugar, and cinnamon in a large mixing bowl. Add the peach slices and toss well. Pile the filling into the baked pie shell.

For the streusel, combine the flour, cinnamon, nutmeg, granulated sugar, and brown sugar in a small mixing bowl. Stir in the walnuts. Add the butter and, using two round-bladed knives, cut into the nut mixture until reduced to small flakes.

Cover the top of the pie evenly but completely with the streusel, pressing it down lightly over the fruit.

Bake in a preheated 375° oven for about 1 hour, until the peaches are tender and the filling bubbles in spots through the streusel, looking like cooked jam.

Transfer to a cooling rack. Serve barely warm or at room temperature.

Deep-Dish Gingered Peach Pie

3 tablespoons cornstarch

¾ cup granulated sugar

3 tablespoons light brown sugar, firmly packed

1 teaspoon ground ginger

¼ teaspoon ground mace

2 tablespoons chopped crystallized ginger

2 tablespoons golden raisins, plumped in ¼ cup boiling water for 1 minute, drained and dried

6 cups peeled, pitted and sliced peaches (about 7 to 8 large peaches), tossed in 1 tablespoon freshly squeezed lemon juice

For this pie, crystallized and ground ginger, raisins, sugar, and cornstarch are folded into ripe peach slices to make a fragrant deep-dish filling. When baked, peaches turn into a lightly thickened compote.

One of summer's pleasures is making and eating this pie —breaking through a flaky top crust, spooning out warm, spiced peaches, and devouring it with clouds of whipped cream.

———◆◆◆———

Blend together the cornstarch, granulated sugar, light brown sugar, ground ginger and mace. Add the chopped ginger, raisins, and peaches, along with any accumulated juice.

Pile the filling in a deep 9-inch pie pan or any other deep-dish ovenproof cooking vessel (round or oval). Dot with butter.

Cover the filling with the round of pie dough, seal, and crimp the edges decoratively, as explained on page 23. Refrigerate for 10 minutes.

For the glaze, brush the top of the pie with milk and sprinkle with sugar. Cut several steam vents, using a sharp paring knife.

Bake in a preheated 425° oven for 25 minutes, reduce the oven temperature to 350°, and continue baking for 20 to 25 minutes longer, or until the crust is golden and the fruit is

1½ tablespoons unsalted butter, cut into bits

one recipe Flaky Pie Crust, prepared for a deep-dish pie cover (page 21)

MILK AND GINGER-SUGAR GLAZE:

2 tablespoons cold milk

1 tablespoon granulated sugar blended with ¼ teaspoon ground ginger

One 9-inch pie

tender. (Test by inserting a toothpick in the vent to feel the consistency of the fruit.)

Transfer to a cooling rack. Serve warm or at room temperature.

Double-Crust Blueberry-Peach Pie

One recipe Flaky Pie
   Crust for a Double-
   Crust Pie (page 30),
   well chilled

¼ cup plus 2 teaspoons
   all-purpose flour

1 cup granulated sugar

¼ teaspoon ground
   cinnamon

¼ teaspoon freshly
   grated nutmeg

3 cups peeled, pitted,
   and sliced peaches
   (about 4 peaches)

1¾ cups blueberries,
   picked over

2 tablespoons unsalted
   butter, cut into bits

1 teaspoon freshly
   squeezed lemon juice,
   strained

During the summer, I always have several kinds of ripe fruit on hand to make an assortment of syrups, glazes, jellies, and preserves to use in cooking and baking throughout the year. One afternoon, I turned an overflow of blueberries and peaches into a double-crust pie, with delicious results. This pie has become a family favorite.

Other than adding a bit of cinnamon and nutmeg to the sugar and flour mixture, I have kept the filling plain to let the taste of each fruit come through.

The blueberry-peach filling can be covered with a lattice top letting patches of fruit show through or can be covered with a plain round of pie dough.

Line a 9-inch pie pan with half of the chilled pie dough following the directions on page 31; refrigerate.

Thoroughly combine the flour, sugar, cinnamon, and nutmeg in a large mixing bowl. Add the peach slices and blueberries. Toss.

Pile the filling in the chilled pie shell, mounding it slightly toward the center. Dot with butter and drizzle with lemon juice. Cover with remaining dough (or weave a latticework top over the filling using the second sheet of dough), seal, and flute the edges decoratively, as explained on page 31. Refrigerate for 10 minutes.

CRACKLE SUGAR GLAZE:

2 tablespoons ice-cold
   water

1 tablespoon granulated
   sugar

One 9-inch pie

Brush the top of the pie with water, sprinkle with sugar, and cut several steam vents using a sharp paring knife.

Bake in a preheated 425° oven for 25 minutes, reduce the oven temperature to 350°, and continue baking for about 30 minutes longer, or until the pastry is golden.

Transfer to a cooling rack. Serve barely warm or at room temperature, with Vanilla Pouring Custard, if you like (page 129).

Baking Note: Pastry cutouts, forming an overlapping cover atop the fruit, may replace the full pie dough cover (see page 32).

Deep-Dish Blueberry Pie

¼ cup all-purpose flour

1 cup granulated sugar

¼ teaspoon freshly grated nutmeg

5 cups blueberries, picked over

2 teaspoons finely grated lemon rind

2 tablespoons unsalted butter, cut into bits

One recipe Flaky Pie Crust, prepared for a deep-dish pie cover (page 21)

MILK AND SUGAR GLAZE:

2 tablespoons cold milk

1 tablespoon granulated sugar

___

One 9-inch pie

Plump blueberries, with a silvery sheen, are one of the easiest summer fruits to turn into a pie. Just pick over the berries for leaves, dump them into a bowl, and toss well in sugar, flour, and nutmeg.

When blueberries are baked in a pie, some of the juices invariably trickle through the steam vents in the top crust. Blueberry pie would not be blueberry pie without them.

Serve large spoonfuls of the filling with some crust attached, partnered with scoops of Double Vanilla Ice Cream, (page 130). I serve this pie in deep plates. I bake it in a deep oval pie dish made of ovenproof porcelain, that I bought in England many years ago. The dish and plates are decorated with clusters of fruit and look beautiful on the table.

Blend together the flour, sugar, and nutmeg in a large mixing bowl. Add the blueberries and lemon rind. Fold the berries through the sugar mixture.

Pile into a deep 9-inch pie pan or any other deep-dish ovenproof cooking vessel (round or oval). Dot with butter.

Cover the filling with the round of pie dough, seal, and crimp the edges decoratively, as explained on page 23. Refrigerate for 10 minutes.

For the glaze, brush the top of the pie with the cold milk and sprinkle with sugar. Cut several steam vents in the top crust with a sharp knife.

Bake in a preheated 425° oven for 20 minutes, reduce the oven temperature to 350°, and continue baking for about 35 minutes longer, or until the top crust is golden. Transfer to a cooling rack. Serve warm or at room temperature.

Spiced Red Plum Pie

One recipe Flaky Pie
  Crust for a Double-
  Crust Pie (page 30),
  well chilled

5 tablespoons all-
  purpose flour

1 cup granulated sugar
  blended with ½
  teaspoon ground
  cinnamon, ½ teaspoon
  freshly grated
  nutmeg, ¼ teaspoon
  ground ginger, and ¼
  teaspoon ground
  allspice

5 cups pitted and sliced
  ripe red plums (about
  11 to 12 plums)

1 tablespoon fresh plum
  syrup, optional (see
  Fresh Fruit Syrups,
  page 37)

1 teaspoon freshly
  squeezed lemon juice

Two sheaths of flaky pie crust hold a solid plum filling flavored with nutmeg, cinnamon, ginger and cloves. It is a pie
to remember when perfect midsummer plums abound.
Choose plump, sweet-scented firm plums. To bring out the
fruit's vivid flavor, I like to top the pie filling with a tablespoon of fresh plum syrup.

   This pie is equally delicious when made with the Italian
prune plums available late summer and early fall. These
small, slightly elongated blue plums need only to be halved
and pitted before tossed with the sugar and spices. The
recipe for Prune Plum Pie, a variation of Spiced Red Plum
Pie, is outlined below.

   For a real treat, serve slices of Spiced Red Plum Pie on
deep dessert plates and pour a big puddle of Vanilla Pouring Custard (page 129) to one side of each slice.

———❖❖❖———

Line a 9-inch pie pan with half of the chilled pie dough
following the directions on page 31; refrigerate.

   Combine the flour and sugar-spice blend in a large mixing bowl. Add the sliced plums and toss.

   Pile the filling in the chilled pie shell, mounding it slightly
toward the center. Drizzle with plum syrup, if desired, and
lemon juice. Cover with remaining dough, seal, and crimp
the edges decoratively, as explained on page 31. Refrigerate
for 10 minutes.

(continued)

CRACKLE SUGAR GLAZE:

2 tablespoons ice-cold
water

1 tablespoon granulated
sugar

One 9-inch pie

For the glaze, brush the top of the pie with water and sprinkle with sugar. Cut several steam vents, using a sharp paring knife.

Bake in a preheated 425° oven for 25 minutes, reduce the oven temperature to 350°, and continue baking for about 30 minutes longer, or until the pastry is golden.

Transfer to a cooling rack. Serve barely warm or at room temperature.

PRUNE PLUM PIE

To make Prune Plum Pie, substitute 5 cups (about 28 to 36) halved and pitted Italian blue prune plums for the red. Very large plums should be pitted and quartered.

Baking Note: A top cover made out of pastry dough cutouts (page 32) may replace the top cover for the pie.

❖❖❖❖❖❖❖❖❖❖❖❖❖❖❖❖❖

Deep-Dish Walnut-Rum-Plum Pie

3 tablespoons cornstarch

1 cup granulated sugar

¼ teaspoon ground
cinnamon

This unusual pie uses a concentrated rum syrup, a number of spices, and chopped walnuts to enrich the sliced plum filling.

Deep-Dish Walnut-Rum-Plum Pie is a splendid dessert to take to a covered dish supper along with a container of Vanilla Pouring Custard (page 129). When the custard is poured over each serving, it mixes with the pie juices, making a delicious combination of fruit and cream.

———❖❖❖———

¼ teaspoon freshly
grated nutmeg

¼ teaspoon ground
allspice

¼ teaspoon ground
ginger

½ cup chopped, lightly
toasted walnuts

6 cups pitted and sliced
red plums (about 14 to
15 plums)

1 teaspoon freshly
squeezed lemon juice

2 tablespoons rum syrup
(see recipe below)

2 tablespoons unsalted
butter, cut into bits

One recipe Flaky Pie
Crust, prepared for a
deep-dish pie cover
(page 21)

MILK AND SUGAR GLAZE:

2 tablespoons cold milk

1 tablespoon granulated
sugar

—————

One 9-inch pie

Blend together the cornstarch, sugar, cinnamon, nutmeg, allspice and ginger. Add the walnuts, plums, and lemon juice. Stir.

Pile the filling in a deep 9-inch pie pan or any other deep-dish ovenproof cooking vessel (round or oval). Drizzle with rum syrup and dot with butter.

Cover the filling with the round of dough, seal, and crimp the edges decoratively, as explained on page 23. Refrigerate for 10 minutes.

For the glaze, brush the top of the pie with milk and sprinkle with sugar. Cut several steam vents in the top crust with a sharp paring knife.

Bake in a preheated 425° oven for 20 minutes, reduce the oven temperature to 350°, and continue baking for 30 to 35 minutes, or until the pastry top is golden.

Transfer to a cooling rack. Serve warm or at room temperature.

RUM SYRUP

To make Rum Syrup, combine ¼ cup dark rum, 1 tablespoon granulated sugar and ¼ cup water in a small saucepan. Cover and cook over low heat for 3 to 4 minutes until the sugar has dissolved. Uncover, bring to a boil over moderately high heat, boil one minute, and cool. Use as directed.

Double-Crust Nectarine Spice Pie

One recipe Flaky Pie
   Crust for a Double-
   Crust Pie (page 30),
   well chilled
¼ cup plus 2 teaspoons
   all-purpose flour
⅞ cup granulated sugar
¼ teaspoon ground
   cinnamon
¼ teaspoon freshly
   grated nutmeg
¼ teaspoon ground
   allspice
5½ cups peeled, pitted,
   and sliced nectarines
   (about 7 to 8
   nectarines)
2 tablespoons nectarine
   syrup, optional (see
   Fresh Fruit Syrups,
   page 37)
2 teaspoons freshly
   squeezed lemon juice,
   strained

The nectarine, often overlooked in favor of its cousin the peach, makes a delicious pie filling. The fruit is sweet smelling and firm, and the peel is easy to remove by dipping the fruit briefly in boiling water.

The pie crust holds nectarines tossed in a mixture of flour, sugar, cinnamon, nutmeg, allspice, and lemon juice. A tablespoon or two of fresh nectarine syrup, if you have it, would heighten the flavor of the fruit.

Serve a slice of pie along with a tall glass of minted iced tea on a hazy summer afternoon, or bring it along to a fried chicken or dinner-on-the-grill supper as your contribution.

———❖❖❖———

Line a 9-inch pie pan with half of the chilled pie dough following the directions on page 31; refrigerate.

Combine the flour, granulated sugar, cinnamon, nutmeg, and allspice in a large mixing bowl. Add the sliced nectarines; toss.

Pile the filling in the chilled pie shell, mounding it slightly toward the center. Drizzle with syrup, if desired, and with lemon juice. Dot with butter. Cover with remaining dough, seal, and crimp the edges decoratively, as explained on page 31. Refrigerate for 10 minutes.

For the glaze, brush the top of the pie with the ice cold water and sprinkle with sugar. Cut several steam vents, using a sharp paring knife.

Bake in a preheated 425° oven for 25 minutes, reduce the

2 tablespoons unsalted
  butter, cut into bits

CRACKLE SUGAR GLAZE:

2 tablespoons ice-cold
  water

1 tablespoon granulated
  sugar

One 9-inch pie

oven temperature to 350°, and continue baking for 25 to 30 minutes longer, or until the pastry top is golden.

Transfer to a cooling rack. Serve barely warm or at room temperature.

Baking Note: A cover of pastry cutouts (page 32) can replace the cover of dough.

Sour Cherry Pie

One recipe Flaky Pie
   Crust for a Double-
   Crust Pie (page 30),
   well chilled

¼ cup plus 2 teaspoons
   all-purpose flour

1¼ cups granulated
   sugar

¼ teaspoon ground
   cinnamon

¼ teaspoon ground
   mace

5 cups sour cherries,
   pitted

2 tablespoons sour
   cherry syrup (see
   Fresh Fruit Syrups,
   page 37)

2 tablespoons unsalted
   butter, cut into bits

MILK AND SUGAR GLAZE:

2 tablespoons cold milk

1 tablespoon granulated
   sugar

One 9-inch pie

Sour cherries make your mouth pucker up when eaten straight, but pitted, tossed with sugar, and baked in a pie shell, their tartness is gentled considerably. The sour cherries I find at a local farm market are a pinkish-red color with a tawny gold cast. They make as good a pie as they do a jelly, glaze, marmalade, or jam.

Sour cherry syrup is called for in this recipe; a few spoonfuls drizzled over the pie filling intensifies the flavor of the cherries as they bake. (If you boil down enough to make a glaze, it becomes a lustrous topping for fresh fruit tarts.)

Line a 9-inch pie pan with half of the chilled pie dough following the directions on page 31; refrigerate.

Combine the flour, sugar, cinnamon, and mace in a large mixing bowl. Add the cherries; toss.

Pile the filling into the chilled pie shell. Drizzle with sour cherry syrup and dot with butter.

Cover with the remaining dough, seal, and crimp the edges decoratively, as explained on page 31. Refrigerate for 10 minutes.

For the glaze, brush the top of the pie with milk and sprinkle with sugar. Cut several steam vents, using a sharp paring knife.

Bake in a preheated 425° oven for 25 minutes, reduce the oven temperature to 350°, and continue baking for 25 to 30 minutes longer, or until the top is golden.

Transfer to a cooling rack. Serve barely warm or at room temperature, with scoops of Double Vanilla Ice Cream, if you like (page 130).

Glazed Yellow Cherry Pie

3 tablespoons cornstarch

1 cup granulated sugar

¼ teaspoon ground cinnamon

⅛ teaspoon each ground allspice and ground cloves

5 cups yellow cherries, pitted

2 teaspoons freshly squeezed lemon juice, strained

One fully baked 9-inch pie shell, made from Flaky Pie Crust (page 21)

2 tablespoons unsalted butter, cut into bits

APPLE JELLY GLAZE:

½ cup apple jelly

2 tablespoons apple juice, or water

2 tablespoons toasted slivered almonds

One 9-inch pie

Plump and sweet yellow cherries are baked in a pie shell topped only with butter; after the filling has thickened, a clear apple jelly glaze is spooned over the top and sprinkled with slivered, lightly toasted almonds, adding a textural edge and a nutty taste.

Yellow cherries make a pretty pie. I often reserve a large handful of cherries with their stems attached to garnish a baked and glazed pie.

Red Bing cherries may be substituted for the yellow cherries, with delicious results.

Blend together the cornstarch, sugar, cinnamon, allspice, and cloves in a large mixing bowl. Add the yellow cherries, and toss. Sprinkle with lemon juice.

Spoon the pie filling into the baked pie shell. Scatter the butter evenly over the top.

Bake in a preheated 375° oven for 40 minutes, or until the filling is bubbly and the cherries are tender.

Transfer to a cooling rack.

To make the glaze: Combine the apple jelly and juice (or water) in a small saucepan. Bring to a simmer over moderate heat. Remove from the heat and spoon the hot glaze over the cherries. Cool completely.

Just before serving, sprinkle the lightly toasted, slivered almonds over the top of the pie.

Deep-Dish Blackberry Pie

5 tablespoons all-
purpose flour

1 cup granulated sugar

6 cups blackberries

2 tablespoons unsalted
butter, cut into bits

One recipe Flaky Pie
Crust, prepared for a
deep-dish pie (page
21)

CRACKLE SUGAR GLAZE:

2 tablespoons ice-cold
water

1 tablespoon granulated
sugar

One 9-inch pie

Sweet and plump blackberries may be turned into jam, mar-malade, and jelly, or used in tarts, cobblers, puddings, and this deep-dish pie.

This is one of the simplest and best-tasting pies I can think of, laden with sweetened berries and nothing more. The blackberries are covered with pastry dough, but you could cut out hearts or diamonds and lay those, overlapping, over the berries.

Deep-Dish Blackberry Pie is scrumptious when served just-out-of-the-oven warm, with scoops of Double Vanilla Ice Cream (page 130).

❖❖❖

Blend together the flour and sugar in a large mixing bowl. Add the berries and toss them well in the sugar mixture.

Pile into a deep 9-inch pie pan, or any other deep-dish ovenproof cooking vessel (round or oval), mounding the berries toward the center. Dot with butter.

Cover the filling with the round of pie dough, seal, and crimp the edges decoratively, as explained on page 23. Refrigerate for 10 minutes.

For the glaze, brush the top of the pie with water and sprinkle with sugar. Cut several steam vents, using a sharp paring knife.

Bake in a preheated 425° oven for 20 minutes, reduce the oven temperature to 350°, and continue baking for 30 to 35 minutes longer, or until the pastry is golden.

Transfer to a cooling rack. Serve warm.

Apple-Raspberry Pie

One recipe Flaky Pie
   Crust for a Double-
   Crust Pie (page 30),
   well chilled
¼ cup all-purpose flour
1 cup granulated sugar
¼ teaspoon freshly
   grated nutmeg
¼ teaspoon ground
   cinnamon
2 cups red raspberries
2⅔ cups peeled, cored,
   and sliced tart cooking
   apples
2 tablespoons red
   raspberry syrup (see
   Fresh Fruit Syrups,
   page 37)
2 tablespoons unsalted
   butter, cut into bits

CREAM AND SUGAR GLAZE:

2 tablespoons cold light
   cream
1 tablespoon granulated
   sugar

One 9-inch pie

For this pie, luscious red raspberries are combined with tart
cooking apples, flour, sugar, and a hint of nutmeg and cinnamon. This flavorsome combination of fruit is enhanced
with some red raspberry syrup drizzled over the filling.

Serve a cold pitcher of minted iced tea with ample slices
of pie and spoonfuls of whipped cream, lightly sweetened
with the raspberry syrup.

———◆◆◆———

Line a 9-inch pie pan with half of the chilled pie dough
following the directions on page 31; refrigerate.

Combine the flour, sugar, nutmeg, and cinnamon in a
large mixing bowl. Pick over the raspberries for any stems.
Add the berries and sliced apples to the flour mixture. Toss
gently.

Pile the filling in the chilled pie shell. Drizzle with raspberry syrup and dot with butter. Cover with remaining
dough, seal, and crimp the edges decoratively, as explained
on page 31. Refrigerate for 10 minutes.

For the glaze, brush the top of the pie with cream and
sprinkle with sugar. Cut several steam vents in the top crust
with a sharp paring knife.

Bake in a preheated 425° oven for 25 minutes, reduce the
oven temperature to 350°, and continue baking for 25 to 30
minutes longer, or until the top is golden.

Transfer to a cooling rack. Serve at room temperature.

Red Raspberry Pie

One recipe Flaky Pie Crust for a Double-Crust Pie (page 30), well chilled

¼ cup plus 2 teaspoons all-purpose flour

1 cup granulated sugar

5 cups red or black raspberries, picked over

2 teaspoons freshly squeezed lemon juice

2 tablespoons unsalted butter, cut into bits

MILK AND SUGAR GLAZE:

2 tablespoons cold milk

1 tablespoon granulated sugar

One 9-inch pie

This is a simple, fresh-tasting pie. Firm red raspberries are tossed in a mixture of sugar, flour, and lemon juice to draw out their flavor. In anticipation of the berry season, when raspberries abound for a few brief weeks, I squirrel away a pile of rolled-out pastry crusts so I can make a pie whenever I bring home pints and quarts of fruit.

From extra cartons of berries, I produce a vibrant raspberry syrup (see Fresh Fruit Syrups, page 37); occasionally, I'll spoon a few tablespoons of the syrup over the pie filling. Black raspberries may be substituted for red raspberries with excellent results.

Line a 9-inch pie pan with half of the chilled pie dough following the directions on page 31; refrigerate.

Blend together the flour and sugar in a large mixing bowl. Add the raspberries and combine gently.

Pile the filling into the chilled pie shell. Drizzle with lemon juice and dot with butter. Cover with the remaining dough, seal, and crimp the edges decoratively, as explained on page 31. Refrigerate for 10 minutes.

For the glaze, brush the top of the pie with milk and sprinkle sugar evenly over the top. Cut several steam vents, using a sharp paring knife.

Bake in a preheated 425° oven for 25 minutes, reduce the oven temperature to 350°, and continue baking for about 25 to 30 minutes longer, or until the top is golden.

Transfer to a cooling rack. Serve at room temperature, with Vanilla Pouring Custard, if you like (page 129).

Fresh Apricot Pie

One recipe Flaky Pie
  Crust for a Double-
  Crust Pie (page 30),
  well chilled

¼ cup all-purpose flour

¾ cup granulated sugar

2 tablespoons light
  brown sugar, firmly
  packed

½ teaspoon freshly
  grated nutmeg

½ teaspoon ground
  cinnamon

4¾ cups pitted and
  quartered ripe
  apricots (about 20
  medium to large
  apricots)

2 tablespoons fresh
  apricot syrup (see
  Fresh Fruit Syrups,
  page 37), optional

2 tablespoons unsalted
  butter, cut into bits

Fresh, fragrant apricots are one of summer's best offerings, and I know of no better way to use them than in this pie— and in fruit syrup, chutney, jelly, and marmalade.

For the pie, the apricots are halved, pitted, and thickly sliced, then tossed with flour, sugar, nutmeg, and cinnamon. Fresh apricot or apricot-plum syrup is a marvelous addition to the pie filling; spoon 2 tablespoons of the syrup over the fruit before covering with the top crust. A cutout pastry cover is a good way to enclose the fruit if you are not using the traditional top crust. I am partial to using scalloped rounds of dough as cutouts; I overlap the rounds slightly, placing them in the center of the pie first, and continue around toward the edge. Serve slices of apricot pie with Vanilla Pouring Custard (page 129), Double Vanilla Ice Cream (page 130), or Vanilla-Scented Whipped Cream (page 131).

———❖❖❖———

Line a 9-inch pie pan with half of the chilled pie dough following the directions on page 31; refrigerate.

Blend together the flour, granulated sugar, light brown sugar, nutmeg, and cinnamon in a large mixing bowl. Add the apricots and toss with the sugar and spice mixture.

Spoon the filling into the chilled pie shell, mounding it slightly toward the center. Drizzle with apricot syrup, if you are using it, and dot with butter.

Cover the filling with the remaining dough, seal, and crimp the edges decoratively, as explained on page 31. Refrigerate for 10 minutes.

(continued)

Fresh Apricot Pie, continued

CREAM AND SUGAR GLAZE:

2 tablespoons cold heavy
  cream

1 tablespoon granulated
  sugar

_____

One 9-inch pie

For the glaze, brush the top of the pie with cream and sprinkle with sugar. Cut several steam vents in the top crust with a sharp paring knife.

Bake in a preheated 425° oven for 25 minutes, reduce the oven temperature to 350°, and continue baking for 25 to 30 minutes longer, or until the pastry crust is golden.

Transfer to a cooling rack. Serve barely warm or at room temperature.

❖❖❖❖❖❖❖❖❖❖❖❖❖❖❖❖❖

Late Season Green Tomato Pie

One recipe Flaky Pie
  Crust for a Double-
  Crust Pie (page 30),
  well chilled

⅓ cup all-purpose flour

1 cup granulated sugar

¼ teaspoon ground
  cinnamon

¼ teaspoon freshly
  grated nutmeg

For this pie filling, sliced green tomatoes are tossed in a lightly spiced mixture of sugar and flour, piled into an un-baked pie shell, and sealed with a round of dough.

When I am not using the full pastry cover, I top the filling with an overlay of pastry cutouts (see page 32) and apply the Crackle Sugar Glaze (recipe below). I also like to cover the filling with a lattice top made from 2- to 3-inch wide strips of interwoven dough. Serve thick slices of the pie with tall glasses of minted or herbal iced tea.

Line a 9-inch pie pan with half of the chilled pie dough following the directions on page 31; refrigerate.

Combine the flour, granulated sugar, cinnamon, nutmeg,

⅛ teaspoon ground
  cloves

4 cups green tomatoes,
  ¼-inch thick (about 6
  tomatoes)

2 tablespoons dark
  raisins, plumped in
  boiling water for 10
  minutes, drained and
  dried

1 teaspoon finely grated
  lemon rind

2 tablespoons unsalted
  butter, cut into bits

CRACKLE SUGAR GLAZE:

2 tablespoons ice-cold
  water

1 tablespoon granulated
  sugar

One 9-inch pie

and cloves in a large mixing bowl. Add the tomatoes, raisins, and lemon rind and fold into the flour mixture.

Spoon the filling into the chilled pie shell and dot with butter. Cover the filling with the remaining dough, seal, and flute the edges decoratively, as explained on page 31. Refrigerate for 10 minutes.

To glaze, brush the top of the pie with water and sprinkle with sugar. Cut several steam vents in the top crust with a sharp paring knife.

Bake in a preheated 425° oven for 15 minutes, reduce the oven temperature to 350°, and continue baking the pie for about 50 minutes longer, or until the pastry is golden.

Transfer to a cooling rack. Serve at room temperature.

AUTUMN
COUNTRY
PIES

AUTUMN COUNTRY PIES

———◆◆◆———

Double-Crust Apple Pie   62
Apple-Ginger Mincemeat Pie   63
Apple-Pear Pie with Apple Cider Syrup   66
Pear Mincemeat Pie   68
Cinnamon-Pear Pie with Walnut Streusel   69
Spiced Pear-Currant Pie   71
Cranberry-Walnut Mincemeat Pie   72
Golden Pecan Pie   74
Bourbon Pecan Pie   75
Pumpkin Custard Pie   76
Pumpkin Crunch Pie   78
Fresh Sugar Pumpkin Pie   80
Apricot-Yam Pie   81
Orange-Butternut Squash Pie   82
Brandied Golden Acorn Squash Pie   84
Coconut-Walnut-Chocolate-Chip "Candy" Pie   86
Brown Sugar Pie   87

*J*ust about the time children go back to school, I am in the kitchen making batches of Dried Fruit and Spice Mincemeat (page 64) to use in pie fillings with pears, apples, and cranberries and quarts of Apple Cider Syrup (page 65) to splash over pie fillings whose flavor needs intensifying. Apple pies, especially, benefit from being moistened with a little cider syrup.

For sweet custard pies, a staple of the fall pie-baking kitchen, I pick out firm pumpkins, slender yams, and heavy butternut and acorn squash at the market. I steam and mash or puree chunks of the vegetables. From fresh pumpkin puree I make Pumpkin Custard Pie (page 76), Pumpkin Crunch Pie (page 78), and Fresh Sugar Pumpkin Pie (page 80). Golden acorn squash puree gets sweetened, spiced, and bound with cream and eggs to make tender custard pies. These fillings are thick, rich, and generously flavored with cinnamon, allspice, ginger, cloves, and freshly grated nutmeg.

Nuts—walnuts and pecans—are in a few fall country pies. Golden Pecan Pie (page 74) and Bourbon Pecan Pie (page 75) are semi-translucent pies made with plenty of eggs and sweetened with a combination of sugars. In the Coconut-Walnut-Chocolate-Chip "Candy" Pie (page 86), chopped walnuts add body and crunch to a filling made of eggs, butter, sugar, and cream.

These pies are substantial and filling; just out of the oven and warm, they are a real treat in chilly weather.

Double-Crust Apple Pie

One recipe Flaky Pie Crust for a Double-Crust Pie (page 30), well chilled

1 tablespoon plus 1½ teaspoons cornstarch

⅓ cup light brown sugar, firmly packed

⅓ cup granulated sugar

¾ teaspoon ground cinnamon

¼ teaspoon freshly grated nutmeg

4 cups peeled, cored, and sliced tart cooking apples (about 5 large apples), tossed in 1 tablespoon freshly squeezed lemon juice

1½ tablespoons cold unsalted butter, cut into bits

MILK AND SUGAR GLAZE:

2 tablespoons cold milk

1 tablespoon granulated sugar

One 9-inch pie

A barely warm helping of apple pie, with a dip of ice cream to one side, is comforting. In my kitchen, making a Double-Crust Apple Pie has become an autumn ritual, along with bottling loads of apple cider syrup and simmering pots full of apple butter and applesauce.

The top of the pie may be etched in a whimsical "spider-web" pattern by using the tip of a skewer to draw the design on the pastry round before covering the pie. Or apply apple-shaped pastry cutouts to the top just before it is baked.

Line a 9-inch pie pan with half of the chilled pie dough following the directions on page 31; refrigerate.

Combine the cornstarch, light brown sugar, granulated sugar, cinnamon, and nutmeg in a large mixing bowl. Blend well. Add the sliced apples and toss.

Spoon the filling into the chilled pie shell, mounding it slightly toward the center. Dot with butter. Cover with remaining dough, seal, and crimp edges decoratively, as explained on page 31. Refrigerate for 10 minutes.

For the glaze, brush the top of the pie with milk and sprinkle with sugar. Cut several steam vents in the top crust with a sharp paring knife.

Bake in a preheated 425° oven for 10 minutes, reduce the oven temperature to 350°, and continue baking for 40 minutes longer, or until the pastry is golden.

Transfer to a cooling rack. Serve warm or at room temperature, accompanied by Vanilla Pouring Custard (page 129), Double Vanilla Ice Cream (page 130), or Vanilla-Scented Whipped Cream (page 131).

❖❖❖❖❖❖❖❖❖❖❖❖❖❖

Apple-Ginger Mincemeat Pie

One recipe Flaky Pie
Crust for a Double-
Crust Pie (page 30),
well chilled

2 tablespoons cornstarch
blended with 1
tablespoon light
brown sugar, firmly
packed

4 cups peeled, cored,
and cubed tart
cooking apples

1 cup Dried Fruit and
Spice Mincemeat
(page 64)

½ cup chopped walnuts

¼ cup ginger, jarred in
syrup, drained and
chopped

1 tablespoon cold unsalted
butter, cut into bits

CRACKLE SUGAR GLAZE:

2 tablespoons ice-cold
water

1 tablespoon granulated
sugar

One 9-inch pie

Once you've made a batch of my Dried Fruit and Spice
Mincemeat—a luxurious thing to have on hand—you can
make all kinds of fall and winter pies. The fruit available
from September through February marries beautifully with
the rich, dark mincemeat.

This home-style pie is a mixture of mincemeat, chopped
walnuts, and ginger preserved in syrup, plus a good quantity of apples. The apples are sweetened by the mincemeat's
syrup and the ginger.

Triangular pieces are delicious with spoonfuls of softly
whipped cream sweetened with some syrup drained from
the ginger; use about 2 tablespoons of syrup to flavor 1 cup
heavy cream.

Line a 9-inch pie pan with half of the chilled pie dough
following the directions on page 31; refrigerate.

Place the cornstarch-brown sugar blend in a large mixing
bowl. Stir in the apples, mincemeat, walnuts, and ginger.
Pile the mixture into the chilled pie shell and dot with butter. Cover with remaining dough, seal, and crimp the edges
decoratively, as explained on page 31. Refrigerate for 10
minutes.

To glaze, brush the top of the pie with water and sprinkle
with the granulated sugar. Cut several steam vents, using a
sharp paring knife.

Bake in a preheated 425° oven for 20 minutes, reduce the
oven temperature to 350°, and continue baking for about
30 to 35 minutes longer, until the pastry is golden.

Transfer to a cooling rack. Serve at room temperature.

Dried Fruit and Spice Mincemeat

1½ cups dark raisins

1½ cups golden raisins

1½ cups dried currants

1½ cups dried peaches, cut into large dice

1½ cups dried apricots, cut into large dice

1½ cups pitted dates, cut into large dice

1½ teaspoons ground cinnamon

½ teaspoon freshly grated nutmeg

¼ teaspoon ground allspice

¼ teaspoon ground ginger

⅓ cup dark corn syrup

1¼ cups dark rum

¾ cup light brown sugar, firmly packed

¼ cup Apple Cider Syrup (see recipe below), optional

This is an elegant, yet quick-to-prepare, mincemeat which uses a full range of dried fruit. Peaches and apricots contribute tanginess, golden raisins and currants provide sweetness, and dates give a honey-like richness.

The mincemeat is especially nice to have on hand for adding a remarkable depth to fruited pie fillings. I also like to use it as a filling for crepes, and sometimes incorporate several tablespoons into a stuffing for Cornish hens or the holiday turkey. It is a blend of mincemeat that bolsters the taste of apples and cranberries, too.

This is a satisfying mincemeat to make. The procedure does not require unlimited hours stirring a bubbling kettle. It's just a matter of boiling a sweet rum and spice liquid and pouring it over the fruit. The fruit plumps in the hot solution, absorbing the spicy syrup.

Jarred, this mincemeat has a long lifespan—about a year —in the refrigerator, where it will continue to mellow. Dried Fruit and Spice Mincemeat makes a dandy bread-and-butter hostess gift for a friend who likes to cook. For gift giving, pack the mincemeat into pretty glass jars up to ¼ inch from the top. Cut a round of heavy brown paper to fit neatly on top of the mincemeat and moisten both sides with rum. Press the disc on top of the mincemeat and seal with the lid. The rum-charged circle will keep the mincemeat flavored throughout the year.

Combine the dark and golden raisins, currants, peaches, apricots, and dates in a large mixing bowl; set aside.

2 cups apple juice
7 tablespoons unsalted
  butter

─────────────

About 11 cups

Put the cinnamon, nutmeg, allspice, and ginger in a large nonreactive saucepan. Stir in the corn syrup, rum, light brown sugar, apple cider syrup (if desired), and apple juice. Add the butter. Bring the mixture to a boil over moderate heat. Boil for 3 minutes. Pour the hot liquid over the dried fruit; stir. Cool to room temperature.

When cooled completely, pour into clean glass jars, seal tightly, and refrigerate.

Apple Cider Syrup

To make a quart jug of Apple Cider Syrup, boil 1 gallon pure, unfiltered apple cider until reduced by half. Add ½ cup light corn syrup, stir well to dissolve. Continue to boil until reduced to 4 cups. Cool to room temperature. Strain through a sieve lined with a double thickness of finely meshed cheesecloth, pour into a bottle, cap tightly, and refrigerate. The syrup will keep indefinitely.

Apple cider syrup adds a concentrated apple flavor to the mincemeat, which I find delightful. If you have a little extra time, I think you will find it well worth making.

Apple-Pear Pie with Apple Cider Syrup

One recipe Flaky Pie Crust for a Double-Crust Pie (page 30), well chilled

2 tablespoons plus 2 teaspoons cornstarch

⅓ cup light brown sugar, firmly packed

⅓ cup granulated sugar

¼ teaspoon ground cinnamon

¼ teaspoon freshly grated nutmeg

¼ teaspoon ground allspice

2 cups peeled, cored and sliced tart cooking apples (about 3 medium-size)

2 cups peeled, cored, and sliced just-ripe pears, preferably D'Anjou (about 3 medium-size)

This fresh fruit pie uses the best of the fall market stand—tart cooking apples and ripe pears. For this pie, I like the combination of just ripe D'Anjou pears and crisp Jonathan apples. Light brown and granulated sugars sweeten the filling, giving it a soft caramel flavor.

I have found that a small amount of concentrated fruit syrup can make a simple pie filling taste extraordinary. Syrups heighten the natural fragrance of the fruit, and they are simple and rewarding to make. Here, I am fond of using a few tablespoons of Apple Cider Syrup (page 65) to intensify the flavor of the apples and pears. If you don't have any, simmer ½ teaspoon light corn syrup in 3 tablespoons apple cider or apple juice until reduced to 2 tablespoons, remove from the heat, and cool completely. When the syrup has cooled to room temperature, spoon it over the apple and pear filling.

———❖❖❖———

Line a 9-inch pie pan with half of the chilled pie dough following the directions on page 31; refrigerate.

Combine the cornstarch, light brown sugar, granulated sugar, cinnamon, nutmeg, and allspice in a large mixing bowl. Add the apples and pears; toss. Pile the filling in the chilled pie shell, mounding it slightly toward the center. Drizzle with apple cider syrup and dot with butter. Cover the pie filling with the remaining dough, seal, and crimp the edges decoratively, as explained on page 31. Refrigerate for 10 minutes.

2 tablespoons Apple
   Cider Syrup (page 65)
2 tablespoons cold
   unsalted butter, cut
   into cubes

MILK AND SUGAR GLAZE:

2 tablespoons cold milk
1 tablespoon granulated
   sugar

One 9-inch pie

For the glaze, brush the top of the pie with milk and
sprinkle with sugar. Cut several steam vents, using a sharp
paring knife.

Bake in a preheated 425° oven for 10 minutes, reduce the
oven temperature to 350°, and continue baking the pie for
40 minutes longer, or until the pastry top is golden.

Transfer to a cooling rack. Serve barely warm or at room
temperature.

Pear Mincemeat Pie

One recipe Flaky Pie Crust for a Double-Crust Pie (page 30), well chilled

3 tablespoons cornstarch

¼ cup granulated sugar, or Vanilla-Flavored Sugar (page 107)

½ teaspoon ground cinnamon

¼ teaspoon freshly grated nutmeg

⅔ cup Dried Fruit and Spice Mincemeat (page 64)

5 cups peeled, cored, and sliced firm but ripe pears (about 6 pears)

½ cup chopped walnuts

This not-too-sweet pie is a lovely late fall dessert, perfect for when we begin to crave the flavors of ripe pears and rum-charged mincemeat. It is quick to put together, providing you've hoarded away a few jars of mincemeat.

The dried fruit mincemeat, which is swirled through the pears, is made of dark and light raisins, currants, peaches, apricots, and dates, as well as a wealth of spices. Its sweeteners (corn syrup, brown sugar, and apple juice) also complement the flavor of the sturdy fall fruit.

There are several ways to craft the top crust for the pie: You can use a solid cover, brush it with milk, and sprinkle with sugar. Or, you can weave a latticework cover (page 33) over the filling, exposing little windows of mincemeat. Finally, you can form a pastry lid from cutouts according to the directions on page 32.

Line a 9-inch pie pan with half of the chilled pie dough following the directions on page 31; refrigerate.

Combine the cornstarch and granulated or vanilla-flavored sugar in a large mixing bowl. The mixture should look like a very fine powder. Blend in the cinnamon and nutmeg. Add the mincemeat, sliced pears, and walnuts; fold in gently.

Spoon the filling into the chilled pie shell, mounding it slightly toward the center. Cover with the remaining dough, seal, and crimp the edges decoratively, as explained on page 31. Refrigerate for 10 minutes.

MILK AND SUGAR GLAZE:

2 tablespoons cold milk

1 tablespoon granulated
sugar

One 9-inch pie

For the glaze, brush the top of the pie with milk and sprinkle with the granulated sugar. Cut several steam vents, using a sharp paring knife.

Bake in a preheated 425° oven for 20 minutes, reduce the oven temperature to 350°, and continue baking for 30 to 35 minutes longer, or until the pastry is golden.

Transfer to a cooling rack. Serve at room temperature, along with generous spoonfuls of Double Vanilla Ice Cream (page 130), if you like.

❖❖❖❖❖❖❖❖❖❖❖❖❖❖❖❖❖❖

Cinnamon-Pear Pie with Walnut Streusel

2 tablespoons plus 2
teaspoons cornstarch

¼ cup plus 1 tablespoon
light brown sugar,
firmly packed

¼ cup granulated sugar

½ teaspoon ground
cinnamon

¼ teaspoon ground
allspice

The "cover" on top of the spiced pear slices is a mantle of crumbs—made of butter, walnuts, flour and sugar. This streusel shelters the pears from the oven's heat, keeping them moist as the pie bakes.

Warm slices of this pie are good with scoops of Double Vanilla Ice Cream (page 130), or drifts of Vanilla-Scented Whipped Cream (page 131) sweetened with 1½ tablespoons liquid brown sugar or maple syrup instead of confectioners' sugar.

————❖❖❖————

Blend together the cornstarch, brown sugar, granulated sugar, cinnamon, and allspice in a large mixing bowl. Add

(continued)

5 cups peeled, cored, and sliced firm but ripe pears (about 6 pears), tossed in 1 tablespoon freshly squeezed lemon juice

One fully baked 9-inch pie shell, made from one recipe Flaky Pie Crust (page 21)

WALNUT STREUSEL TOPPING:

½ cup all-purpose flour

¼ cup granulated sugar

2 tablespoons light brown sugar, firmly packed

¼ teaspoon ground cinnamon

¼ teaspoon freshly grated nutmeg

⅓ cup chopped walnuts

4 tablespoons (½ stick) cold unsalted butter, cut into cubes

One 9-inch pie

the pears with any accumulated liquid. Toss gently. Pile the filling into the pie shell, mounding it slightly toward the center.

To make the topping, blend together the flour, granulated sugar, light brown sugar, cinnamon, nutmeg, and walnuts in a small mixing bowl. Add the butter and, using two round-bladed knives, cut into the flour mixture until it resembles a very coarse meal.

Cover the pie evenly and completely with the streusel, pressing it down gently.

Bake in a preheated 375° oven for about 1 hour, or until the pears are tender and the filling bubbles through the topping in spots, looking like cooked jam.

Transfer to a cooling rack. Serve warm or at room temperature.

Spiced Pear-Currant Pie

One recipe Flaky Pie Crust for a Double-Crust Pie (page 30), well chilled

¼ cup all-purpose flour

⅓ cup light brown sugar, firmly packed

⅓ cup granulated sugar

½ teaspoon ground cinnamon

½ teaspoon freshly grated nutmeg

¼ teaspoon ground ginger

¼ teaspoon ground allspice

Pinch of salt

5 cups peeled, cored, and sliced firm but ripe pears (about 6 pears), tossed in 1½ tablespoons freshly squeezed lemon juice

¼ cup dried currants

2 tablespoons unsalted butter, cut into bits

A mound of sweetened sliced and spiced pears, dotted here and there with currants, is just about as perfect a filling for a cold weather pie as you could imagine. The pears bake to a buttery tenderness underneath a tent of pastry dough.

For this double-crust pie, I like to flute the edges in a deep scallop pattern and apply five small pear-shaped pastry cutouts in a ring close to the edge of the pie. This adds a charming finishing touch and hints at what's in the filling.

Line a 9-inch pie pan with half of the chilled pie dough, following the directions on page 31; refrigerate.

Combine the flour, brown sugar, granulated sugar, cinnamon, nutmeg, ginger, allspice, and salt in a large mixing bowl. Stir well. Add the sliced pears and currants; toss gently.

Spoon the filling into the chilled pie shell, heaping it in a mound. Dot with butter. Cover with the remaining round of dough, seal, and flute the edges decoratively, as explained on page 31. Refrigerate for 10 minutes.

To glaze the pie, brush the top crust with the ice cold water. Press on any pastry cutouts, if you are using them, and brush with water. Sprinkle with sugar. Cut several steam vents, using a sharp paring knife.

Bake in a preheated 425° oven for 20 minutes, reduce the oven temperature to 350°, and continue baking for 35 minutes longer, or until the top is golden.

(continued)

CRACKLE SUGAR GLAZE:

2 tablespoons ice-cold water

1 tablespoon granulated sugar

One 9-inch pie

Transfer to a cooling rack. Serve barely warm or at room temperature with Vanilla-Scented Whipped Cream (page 131) if you like.

Baking Note: If the dried currants are not as supple and moist as they should be, heat ½ cup apple juice in a small saucepan until hot. Remove from heat, add the currants, and steep for 5 minutes. Drain well and dry on several thicknesses of paper toweling. They are now ready to be used.

❖❖❖❖❖❖❖❖❖❖❖❖❖❖❖❖❖❖

Cranberry-Walnut Mincemeat Pie

One recipe Flaky Pie Crust for a Double-Crust Pie (page 30), well chilled

2 tablespoons plus 2 teaspoons cornstarch blended with 2 tablespoons granulated sugar

3 cups Dried Fruit and Spice Mincemeat (page 64)

Cranberries provide just the right tart edge to mincemeat. Just about the time they flood the produce bins, we're well into fall with the season's mincemeat already made.

Line a 9-inch pie pan with half of the chilled pie dough following the directions on page 31; refrigerate.

Put the cornstarch-sugar blend in a large mixing bowl with the mincemeat; stir. Add the cranberry preserve and walnuts and fold through.

Spoon the filling into the chilled pie shell. Cover with the remaining dough, seal, and crimp the edges decoratively as explained on page 31. Refrigerate for 10 minutes.

To glaze, brush the top of the pie with cold water and sprinkle with sugar. Cut several steam vents, using a sharp paring knife.

1 cup Cranberry
   Preserve, preferably
   homemade (see recipe
   below)
1 cup lightly toasted,
   coarsely chopped
   walnuts

CRACKLE SUGAR GLAZE:

2 tablespoons ice-cold
   water
1 tablespoon granulated
   sugar.

One 9-inch pie

Bake in a preheated 425° oven for 15 minutes, reduce the oven temperature to 350°, and continue baking for about 35 minutes, or until the pastry top is golden.

Transfer to a cooling rack. Serve at room temperature, with some Vanilla-Scented Whipped Cream (page 131) on the side, if you like.

Cranberry Preserve

Homemade cranberry preserve, one that's not too thick, makes the best-tasting pie. To make this condiment, combine 1¼ cups water and 1 cup granulated sugar which has been blended with ½ teaspoon ground cinnamon, ¼ teaspoon ground allspice, and ¼ teaspoon ground ginger in a large nonreactive pot. Add 2 tablespoons orange juice and 1 tablespoon finely grated orange rind. Cover and cook over low heat until the sugar dissolves. Uncover, add one 12-ounce bag fresh cranberries (washed and picked over), and bring to a boil while stirring. When the berries begin to burst rapidly, cook about 45 seconds to 1 minute longer, then remove from the heat. Cool this softly thickened preserve to room temperature, transfer to a container, cover airtight, and refrigerate. The preserve will keep for at least 6 weeks.

Golden Pecan Pie

4 extra-large eggs, at room temperature

1 cup granulated sugar

½ cup plus 1 tablespoon light brown sugar, firmly packed

¼ teaspoon salt

8 tablespoons (¼ pound or 1 stick) unsalted butter, melted and cooled

1¾ cups pecan pieces, coarsely chopped

One fully baked 9-inch pie shell, made from one recipe Flaky Pie Crust (page 21)

One 9-inch pie

Th.... .... eggs and butter, and thoroughly loaded with pecans. I love to use nutmeats from freshly cracked pecans (and from walnuts, too, for that matter) because I know they will be crisp and lightly oily. As a child, I was in charge of cracking all the nuts for my mother's fruitcake, so cracking nuts is a natural part of the baking process for me.

The simple, sweet filling is easily mixed in a batter bowl; after baking it becomes partially translucent, quivery, and jelly-like, interspersed with pecans.

A warm slice of Golden Pecan Pie with a hot cup of tea or coffee is a fine afternoon treat.

———✦✦✦———

Beat the eggs in a large mixing bowl. Blend in the granulated and light brown sugar. Stir in the salt, butter, and pecans.

Pour the filling into the baked pie shell. Bake in a preheated 425° oven for 10 minutes, reduce the oven temperature to 350°, and continue baking for 25 minutes longer, or until the top is set and a knife inserted 1 to 2 inches from the center withdraws clean.

Transfer to a cooling rack. Serve barely warm, or at room temperature, accompanied by Vanilla-Scented Whipped Cream (page 131).

Bourbon Pecan Pie

4 extra-large eggs, at room temperature

¾ cup dark brown sugar, firmly packed

¾ cup dark corn syrup

¼ teaspoon salt

1 tablespoon bourbon

2 teaspoons pure vanilla extract

6 tablespoons unsalted butter, melted and cooled

1¾ cups pecan pieces, coarsely chopped

One fully baked 9-inch pie shell, made from one recipe Flaky Pie Crust (page 21)

One 9-inch pie

This is a dandy pie to carry along to a fall picnic, or to serve as one among many desserts at a holiday meal or celebration. The little swig of bourbon does wonders for the pecans, and that taste may be repeated in an accompaniment. Try blending 2 teaspoons of a good-quality bourbon into the Vanilla Pouring Custard (page 129) or Vanilla-Scented Whipped Cream (page 131) just before serving.

Beat the eggs in a large mixing bowl. Blend in the dark brown sugar and corn syrup. Stir in the salt, bourbon, vanilla, butter, and pecans.

Pour the filling into the baked pie shell. Bake in a preheated 425° oven for 10 minutes, reduce the oven temperature to 350°, and continue baking for 25 minutes longer, or until the top is set and a knife inserted 1 to 2 inches from the center withdraws clean.

Transfer to a cooling rack. Serve warm or at room temperature.

Pumpkin Custard Pie

½ cup light brown sugar, firmly packed

½ cup granulated sugar

1 tablespoon all-purpose flour

1 teaspoon ground cinnamon

¼ teaspoon freshly grated nutmeg

¼ teaspoon ground allspice

3 extra-large eggs, at room temperature

2 cups Fresh Pumpkin Puree (see below), or one 1-pound can solid-pack pumpkin puree (not pumpkin pie filling)

1 cup heavy cream, at room temperature

½ cup light cream, at room temperature

2 teaspoons pure vanilla extract

This pumpkin pie is one that's always requested for Thanksgiving—it's a light custard made from pumpkin puree, a few spices, eggs, and cream.

I usually make an extra batch of dough, roll it thinly, and stamp out turkey shapes using a cookie cutter. While I prebake the pie crust, I bake the pastry turkeys alongside. After the pie has been baked and cooled, I place a ring of turkeys around the perimeter, for a festive look. Maple leaves cut out of dough also look pretty edging the baked pie.

Combine the light brown sugar, granulated sugar, flour, cinnamon, nutmeg, and allspice in a large mixing bowl. Add the eggs, one at a time, blending well after each addition. Beat in the pumpkin puree. Stir in the heavy cream, light cream, and vanilla.

Pour the filling into the baked pie shell. Bake in a preheated 400° oven for 10 minutes, reduce the oven temperature to 325°, and continue baking for about 40 minutes or until set and a knife inserted 1 to 2 inches from the center withdraws clean.

Transfer to a cooling rack. Serve tepid or at room temperature, with dollops of Vanilla-Scented Whipped Cream (page 131).

One fully baked deep
  10-inch pie shell,
  made from one recipe
  Flaky Pie Crust (page
  21)

One 10-inch pie

Fresh Pumpkin Puree

Freshly cooked and pureed pumpkin makes a delightful pie filling. The puree is easy to make: Cut a pumpkin into thick wedges, scrape away the seeds and then cut into large chunks. Steam until tender, cool, and scrape the flesh away from the skin. Discard the skin. Puree the flesh, in batches, in a food processor fitted with the steel knife, or through a food mill fitted with the fine disk. Once the puree has cooled completely, it is ready to be used in a pie filling.

Pumpkin Crunch Pie

½ cup granulated sugar

1 tablespoon all-purpose flour

½ teaspoon ground cinnamon

½ teaspoon freshly grated nutmeg

¼ teaspoon ground allspice

⅛ teaspoon ground cloves

2 extra-large eggs, plus 1 extra-large egg yolk, at room temperature

2 cups Fresh Pumpkin Puree (page 77), or 1-pound can solid-pack pumpkin puree (not pumpkin pie filling)

1 cup light cream, at room temperature

1 teaspoon pure vanilla extract

One fully baked deep 9-inch pie shell, made from one recipe Flaky Pie Crust (page 21)

This pie's topping consists of a brittle "crunch"—a crumble of brown sugar, butter, and walnuts that crowns a simple pumpkin base. This pie is a delightful change from the more traditional pumpkin pies, and the candy-nut topping can be applied over almost any squash pie with a thick and substantial filling.

This topping is a good way to use up small odd lots of nuts. You may vary the taste of the topping by substituting chopped pecans or macadamia nuts for the walnuts.

Combine the granulated sugar, flour, cinnamon, nutmeg, allspice, and cloves in a large mixing bowl. Add the eggs, one at a time, blending well after each addition. Beat in the egg yolk. Beat in the pumpkin puree. Stir in the light cream and vanilla.

Pour the filling into the baked pie shell. Bake in a preheated 425° oven for 10 minutes, reduce the oven temperature to 375°, and continue baking for 10 minutes longer.

CRUNCH TOPPING

While the pie is baking, make the crunch topping. Put the brown sugar in a small mixing bowl. Scatter over it the cubes of butter and chopped walnuts. Using two round-bladed knives, cut the butter into the sugar and walnuts until reduced to small flakes. Stir in the cinnamon and nutmeg.

Remove the pie from the oven, quickly sprinkle the topping in an even layer, and return to the oven. Reduce the

CRUNCH TOPPING:

¼ cup light brown sugar,
  firmly packed

4 tablespoons (½ stick)
  cold unsalted butter,
  cut into cubes

¾ cup chopped walnuts

¼ teaspoon ground
  cinnamon

¼ teaspoon freshly
  grated nutmeg

One 9-inch pie

oven temperature to 350° and continue to bake for about
30 minutes or until set and a knife inserted 1 inch from the
center withdraws clean.

Transfer to a cooling rack. Serve barely warm, or at room
temperature, accompanied by Vanilla-Scented Whipped
Cream (page 131), if you like.

Fresh Sugar Pumpkin Pie

⅔ cup light brown sugar, firmly packed

½ teaspoon ground cinnamon

½ teaspoon freshly grated nutmeg

¼ teaspoon ground cloves

1 tablespoon all-purpose flour

3 extra-large eggs, at room temperature

2 cups Fresh Sugar Pumpkin Puree

1 cup light cream blended with ¼ cup heavy cream, at room temperature

1 tablespoon maple syrup

2 teaspoons pure vanilla extract

2 tablespoons unsalted butter, melted and cooled

One fully baked deep 9-inch pie shell, made from one recipe Flaky Pie Crust (page 21)

One 9-inch pie

A small, sweet baby pumpkin, affectionately known as a "sugar pumpkin," is esteemed for its thick, meaty flesh, perfect for turning into a puree and using in many pie fillings. This pie makes a handsome finish to a holiday meal.

———❖❖❖———

Blend together the brown sugar, cinnamon, nutmeg, cloves, and flour in a large mixing bowl. Add the eggs, one at a time, blending well after each addition. Beat in the pumpkin puree. Stir in the light- and heavy-cream blend, maple syrup, vanilla, and butter.

Pour the filling into the baked pie shell. Bake in a preheated 400° oven for 10 minutes, reduce the oven temperature to 325°, and continue baking for 35 minutes longer, or until set and a knife inserted about 1 to 2 inches from the center withdraws clean.

Transfer to a cooling rack. Serve at room temperature, with Vanilla Pouring Custard (page 129) or Vanilla-Scented Whipped Cream (page 131), if you like.

Fresh Sugar Pumpkin Puree

Quarter a 2-pound sugar pumpkin, pare it, scoop out the seeds, and cut it into big chunks; the flesh gets steamed until tender (about 15 to 20 minutes), scraped away from the skin, and pureed in the bowl of a food processor fitted with the steel knife.

Apricot-Yam Pie

½ cup light brown sugar, firmly packed

½ cup granulated sugar

1 tablespoon all-purpose flour

½ teaspoon ground cinnamon

¼ teaspoon ground ginger

¼ teaspoon ground allspice

3 extra-large eggs, at room temperature

2 cups fresh Yam Puree

1 cup heavy cream, at room temperature

½ cup good-quality unfiltered apricot nectar

3 tablespoons unsalted butter, melted and cooled

One fully baked 10-inch pie shell, made from one recipe Flaky Pie Crust (page 21)

One 10-inch pie

This is a sweet, mellow pie made with pureed yams and enhanced with a splash of unfiltered apricot nectar. Good-quality unfiltered nectars can be purchased at a natural foods store. The nectar contributes a fruity undertone to the pie. Peach or plum nectar can be substituted for the apricot, as can any fairly dense, concentrated fruit syrup. If you use a fruit syrup, reduce the amount of granulated sugar in this recipe to ¼ cup.

Blend together the brown sugar, granulated sugar, flour, cinnamon, ginger, and allspice in a large mixing bowl. Add the eggs, one at a time, blending well after each addition. Blend in the yam puree. Stir in the heavy cream, apricot nectar, and butter.

Pour the filling into the baked pie shell. Bake in a preheated 350° oven for 45 minutes, or until set and a knife inserted 1 to 2 inches from the center withdraws clean.

Transfer to a cooling rack. Serve barely warm, or at room temperature, with Vanilla-Scented Whipped Cream (page 131), if you like.

Yam Puree

To make 2 cups of yam puree, steam 3 large yams (about 1½ to 1¾ pounds) until tender. When cool enough to handle, peel away the jackets and cut the flesh into chunks. Puree in the bowl of a food processor fitted with the steel knife, or pass through a food mill fitted with the fine disk. Cool completely before using.

Orange-Butternut Squash Pie

¾ cup light brown sugar, firmly packed

1 tablespoon all-purpose flour

½ teaspoon ground cinnamon

½ teaspoon ground ginger

¼ teaspoon freshly grated nutmeg

Pinch of salt

3 extra-large eggs, at room temperature

2 cups fresh Butternut Squash Puree

1 tablespoon finely grated orange rind

1 teaspoon pure orange extract

2 tablespoons good-quality orange cut marmalade

1 cup heavy cream, at room temperature

Pureed butternut squash, orange peel, and orange marmalade are combined with the usual brown sugar, spices, eggs, and cream to make a sweet vegetable custard pie.

When fall and winter squash proliferate, it's a good idea to steam several pounds at once, puree the flesh, and divide into 2-cup portions for use in pies throughout the season. Spoon the puree into heavy-duty freezer containers, press a double thickness of plastic wrap onto the surface, cover tightly, cool, and freeze.

This pie looks pretty when baked in a shell with a deeply ruffled border; make a few autumn leaves out of pastry dough, bake them, and place atop the filling when the pie emerges from the oven.

A slice of this pie is delicious when accompanied by a hot cup of orange herbal tea.

Blend together the brown sugar, flour, cinnamon, ginger, nutmeg, and salt in a large mixing bowl. Add the eggs, one at a time, blending well after each addition. Beat in the squash puree. Stir in the orange rind, extract, marmalade, heavy cream, and light cream.

Pour the filling into the baked pie shell. Bake in a preheated 350° oven for 45 minutes, or until the filling has set and a knife inserted 1 to 2 inches from the center withdraws clean.

Transfer to a cooling rack. Serve at room temperature.

½ cup light cream, at
   room temperature
One fully baked 10-inch
   pie shell, made from
   one recipe Flaky Pie
   Crust (page 21)

One 10-inch pie

Butternut Squash Puree

To make 2 cups of butternut squash puree, halve one 2
pound butternut squash. Scoop away the seeds, cut into
large chunks, and steam until tender, about 15 to 20 minutes. Cool slightly, scrape the flesh from the skin, and puree
in the bowl of a food processor fitted with the steel knife, or
through a food mill fitted with the fine disk. Cool completely before using.

Brandied Golden Acorn Squash Pie

½ cup light brown sugar, firmly packed

2 tablespoons granulated sugar

½ teaspoon ground cinnamon

½ teaspoon freshly grated nutmeg

¼ teaspoon ground ginger

⅛ teaspoon ground mace

3 extra-large eggs, at room temperature

2 cups fresh Golden Acorn Squash Puree

1 cup heavy cream, at room temperature

¼ cup light cream, at room temperature

2 tablespoons brandy

1 teaspoon pure vanilla extract

The flesh of the golden acorn squash turns tender and buttery when steamed and pureed. Brandy adds a little kick to the filling, which bakes into an exceptionally tender, lightly sweetened custard.

I have enjoyed slices of this pie on snowy evenings sitting opposite a roaring fire, and on cool afternoons as a teatime sweet.

Blend together the brown sugar, granulated sugar, cinnamon, nutmeg, ginger, and mace in a large mixing bowl. Add the eggs, one at a time, blending well after each addition. Beat in the squash puree. Stir in the heavy cream, light cream, brandy, vanilla, and melted butter.

Pour the filling into the baked pie shell. Bake in a preheated 400° oven for 10 minutes, reduce the oven temperature to 325°, and continue baking for about 35 to 40 minutes longer, or until set and a knife inserted 1 to 2 inches from the center withdraws clean.

Transfer to a cooling rack. Serve at room temperature.

2 tablespoons unsalted
butter, melted and
cooled

One fully baked 10-inch
pie shell, made from
one recipe Flaky Pie
Crust (page 21)

One 10-inch pie

Golden Acorn Squash Puree

To make 2 cups of golden acorn squash puree, halve 2
pounds of acorn squash. Scoop out the seeds, cut the flesh
into large chunks, and steam until tender, about 15 to 20
minutes. Cool slightly, scrape the flesh from the skin, and
puree in the bowl of a food processor fitted with the steel
knife. Or, pass the squash through a food mill fitted with
the fine disk. Cool completely before using.

Coconut-Walnut-Chocolate-Chip "Candy" Pie

¾ cup all-purpose flour

Pinch of salt

3 extra-large eggs, at room temperature

1 cup granulated sugar

3 tablespoons light brown sugar, firmly packed

5 tablespoons unsalted butter, melted and cooled, blended with 1 tablespoon heavy cream

2 teaspoons pure vanilla extract

1 cup miniature semi-sweet chocolate chips

1 cup chopped walnuts

1 cup sweetened shredded coconut

One fully baked deep 9-inch pie shell, made from one recipe Flaky Pie Crust (page 21)

One deep 9-inch pie

This confection-like pie is my version of one my grandmother Lilly used to make—it's thick with shredded coconut, chopped walnuts, and miniature chocolate chips. Miniature chips were not available during grandma's time; she chopped up bittersweet chocolate candy bars bought at her local coffee, tea, and spice shop in Georgetown. This pie is best served barely warm, with vanilla ice cream, when it tastes like a soft, faintly caramel-flavored chocolate and nut candy bar.

Sift the flour and salt together onto a sheet of waxed paper; set aside.

Beat the eggs in a large mixing bowl. Beat in the granulated sugar, light brown sugar, butter–heavy-cream blend, and vanilla. Add flour and beat in. Stir in the chocolate chips, walnuts, and coconut.

Pour the filling into the baked pie shell. Bake in a preheated 350° oven for 1 hour, or until it is set and a knife inserted 2 inches from the center has only a few moist particles clinging to it.

Transfer to a cooling rack. Serve warm or at room temperature, with scoops of Double Vanilla Ice Cream (page 130), if you like.

Brown Sugar Pie

1 cup light brown sugar, firmly packed

⅓ cup all-purpose flour

Pinch of salt

1 cup heavy cream

¾ cup light cream

2 teaspoons pure vanilla extract

One fully baked 9-inch pie shell, made from one recipe Flaky Pie Crust (page 21)

4 tablespoons (½ stick) unsalted butter, cut into bits

¼ teaspoon freshly grated nutmeg

One 9-inch pie

Creamy and tasting faintly of caramel, this is a rich and satisfying version of a sugar pie. Those who remember it from their childhood will find this homespun variation just as pleasing. I use heavy cream and light cream as the liquid, brown sugar as the sweetener, and flavor it lightly with nutmeg.

This pie should be enjoyed on its own, without further adornment. I like to bake this pie in one of my antique pie tins. In it the pie looks wholesome and fresh and very appealing.

Blend together the light brown sugar, flour, and salt in a small mixing bowl. Pour the heavy cream and light cream into a saucepan, set over moderately high heat, and warm slightly (about 3 to 4 minutes); remove from heat and stir in vanilla.

Sprinkle the sugar-flour mixture evenly on the bottom of the pie shell. Pour the cream-vanilla blend over the sugar mixture.

Dot the top of the pie with the bits of butter. Grate nutmeg over the top of the pie.

Bake in a preheated 350° oven for 50 to 55 minutes, until golden on top.

Transfer to a cooling rack. Serve at room temperature.

WINTER
COUNTRY
PIES

WINTER COUNTRY PIES

———◆◆◆———

Vanilla Custard Pie 92
Coconut Custard Pie 93
Maple Cream Pie 94
Maple-Walnut Pie 95
Old-Fashioned Chocolate Fudge Pie 96
Mile-High Coconut Cream Pie 98
Banana Cream Pie 100
Chocolate Silk Pie 102
Spicy Sweet Potato Pie 103
Apple Streusel Pie 104
Buttermilk Pie 106

*E*very time I do my marketing in winter, I am reminded of the rich array of nuts that can be used in pies. Enormous heaps of nuts are set in large bins or burlap sacks. I buy several pounds at once and, at home, pile the nuts in an old basket or bowl. There they sit ready to be cracked, their nutmeats picked out and chopped. Winter is the time to make use of the plentiful supply of walnuts; once they are cracked, I use the chopped walnuts in Maple-Walnut Pie (page 95), an interesting variation of the translucent pecan pie. I also combine chopped walnuts with sugar, flour, butter, and spices to make a streusel covering for apple pie.

During winter, I keep cream and eggs on hand for making vanilla, coconut, maple cream, or custard pies. I keep the pantry shelf stacked with squares of unsweetened chocolate for filling an Old-Fashioned Chocolate Fudge Pie (page 96) or Chocolate Silk Pie (page 102); I have bananas ripening at room temperature for slicing into a Banana Cream Pie (page 100); and I make a special trip to a nearby dairy or natural food store to buy fresh buttermilk for my Buttermilk Pie (page 106).

Winter country pies are delicious when served with a steaming pot of tea or coffee, or little cups of espresso at the close of a meal. I also like to accompany slices of pie with large cups of mulled cider or herbal tea for a casual, afternoon tea-and-sweets break.

Vanilla Custard Pie

4 extra-large eggs, at
   room temperature

½ cup granulated sugar

1 cup heavy cream, at
   room temperature

1 cup light cream, at
   room temperature

¼ cup milk, at room
   temperature

2 teaspoons pure vanilla
   extract

One fully baked 9-inch
   pie shell, made from
   one recipe Flaky Pie
   Crust (page 21)

¼ teaspoon freshly
   grated nutmeg

One 9-inch pie

Custard pie is plain and delicate; it's made with fresh eggs and cream set just to the point of perfection. I usually use free-range chicken eggs; the orange-yellow yolks deeply color and enrich the custard and thicken up the filling wonderfully.

For this pie, I like to grate a little nutmeg over the top before baking to enhance the flavor of the custard.

Beat the eggs in a large mixing bowl. Blend in the sugar, heavy cream, light cream, and milk. Stir in the vanilla.

Pour the filling into the baked pie shell and grate the nutmeg evenly over the top. Bake in a preheated 425° oven for 10 minutes, reduce the oven temperature to 325°, and continue baking for 35 minutes longer, or until the filling has set and a knife inserted 2 inches from the center withdraws clean.

Transfer to a cooling rack. Serve warm or at room temperature.

Coconut Custard Pie

4 extra-large eggs, at
  room temperature

½ cup granulated sugar

1 cup heavy cream, at
  room temperature

1 cup light cream, at
  room temperature

2 teaspoons pure
  coconut extract

1 teaspoon pure vanilla
  extract

1 cup sweetened
  shredded coconut

One fully baked 9-inch
  pie shell, made from
  one recipe Flaky Pie
  Crust (page 21)

¼ teaspoon freshly
  grated nutmeg

One 9-inch pie

Coconut Custard Pie is a toothsome variation of a silken custard pie. To make it, you stir a cupful of shredded coconut into the basic egg and cream mixture. This is a nourishing pie with body and substance, perfect to serve on a blustery winter evening with a steaming pot of coffee.

More often than not, I make this pie in an antique pie plate from my collection; the old-fashioned, worn surface produces a golden and flaky crust.

———❖❖❖———

Beat the eggs in a large mixing bowl until combined. Whisk in the sugar, heavy cream, and light cream. Blend in the coconut and vanilla extracts. Stir in the coconut.

Pour the filling into the baked pie shell and grate the nutmeg evenly over the top. Bake in a preheated 425° oven for 10 minutes, reduce the oven temperature to 325°, and continue baking for 35 minutes longer, or until the filling has set and the top is a light golden color. A knife inserted 2 inches from the center of the pie will withdraw clean.

Transfer to a cooling rack. Serve warm or at room temperature.

Maple Cream Pie

1 cup heavy cream

½ cup light cream

Pinch of salt

4 extra-large eggs, at room temperature

2 extra-large egg yolks, at room temperature

¼ cup light brown sugar, firmly packed

¼ cup plus 2 tablespoons good-quality pure maple syrup

2 teaspoons pure maple extract

1 teaspoon pure vanilla extract

One fully baked 9-inch pie shell, made from one recipe Flaky Pie Crust (page 21)

One 9-inch pie

This hearty pie is wonderful to make in the dead of winter when you want a satisfying and smooth-textured sweet. The filling is nothing more than a luxurious blend of maple syrup, cream, eggs, vanilla, and brown sugar, baked in a buttery pie crust.

A narrow ring of chopped, lightly toasted walnuts may be sprinkled around the edge of the baked pie, if you like, for crunch.

———◈◈◈———

Put the heavy cream, light cream, and pinch of salt into a heavy, medium-size saucepan. Place over moderate heat, bring to the scalding point, remove from heat, and set aside.

Beat the eggs and egg yolks in a large mixing bowl until combined. Beat in the brown sugar and maple syrup. Blend in the maple and vanilla extracts. Stir ¼ cup of the scalded cream into the egg yolk mixture. Slowly add the remaining scalded cream to the egg yolk mixture in a thin, steady stream, whisking all the while.

Pour the filling into the baked pie shell. Bake in a preheated 400° oven for 10 minutes, reduce the oven temperature to 325°, and continue baking for about 35 minutes longer, or until the filling has set. The filling will wiggle ever so faintly like a baked custard does, and a knife inserted 2 inches from the center withdraws clean.

Transfer to a cooling rack. Serve barely warm or at room temperature.

Maple-Walnut Pie

3 extra-large eggs, at
  room temperature

⅓ cup light brown sugar,
  firmly packed

2 teaspoons all-purpose
  flour

Pinch of salt

1 cup pure maple syrup

2 teaspoons pure vanilla
  extract

¼ cup heavy cream, at
  room temperature

5 tablespoons unsalted
  butter, melted and
  cooled

1⅓ cups fresh walnuts,
  coarsely chopped

One fully baked 9-inch
  pie shell, made from
  one recipe Flaky Pie
  Crust (page 21)

One 9-inch pie

The earthy flavors of maple syrup and walnuts are combined in this pie filling, which joins together the best qualities of a custard and a translucent pie. Eggs, light brown sugar, maple syrup, vanilla, butter, and walnuts make a fairly rich concoction, reminiscent of the maple-walnut sauce from old-time ice cream parlors.

Warm slices of this pie are luscious when served with espresso or with freshly brewed lemon or English Breakfast tea. I like to offer wedges at a late afternoon tea, or several hours after dinner, when its richness can be appreciated.

Beat the eggs in a large mixing bowl until combined. Combine the brown sugar, flour, and salt; add to the eggs. Beat in the maple syrup, vanilla, and heavy cream. Stir in the butter and walnuts.

Pour the filling into the baked pie shell. Bake in a preheated 425° oven for 10 minutes, reduce the oven temperature to 325°, and continue baking for about 30 minutes, or until set (the center 2 inches will quiver slightly, but the pie will still be baked through). A knife inserted about 2 to 3 inches from the edge of the pie will withdraw clean.

Transfer to a cooling rack. Serve warm, or at room temperature, with spoonfuls of Vanilla-Scented Whipped Cream (page 131), or scoops of vanilla ice cream.

Old-Fashioned Chocolate Fudge Pie

12 tablespoons (¼ pound plus 4 tablespoons or 1½ sticks) unsalted butter, cut into chunks

3 squares (3 ounces) unsweetened chocolate, coarsely chopped

3 extra-large eggs, plus 1 extra-large egg yolk, at room temperature

1½ cups granulated sugar

6 tablespoons all-purpose flour

¼ teaspoon salt

2 teaspoons pure vanilla extract

One fully baked 9-inch pie shell, made from one recipe Flaky Pie Crust (page 21)

I've been baking this dense and rich fudge pie for as long as I can remember. The perfect balance of chocolate to butter to eggs makes this filling firm yet creamy, with an irresistible chocolate flavor.

The fudge filling may be hidden under a thick mantle of whipped cream flavored with vanilla and sweetened with confectioners' sugar. The cream topping becomes a perfect counterpoint to the dreamy filling.

Put the butter and chocolate in a heavy saucepan set over low heat. Cook slowly until melted, stirring occasionally. Set aside to cool.

Beat the eggs and egg yolk in a large mixing bowl until combined. Blend together the sugar, flour, and salt, and beat into the eggs. Whisk in the cooled chocolate and butter. Stir in the vanilla.

Pour the filling into the baked pie shell. Bake in a pre-heated 325° oven for about 40 minutes, or until the filling has just set (small bubbles may appear over the surface of the baked pie). A knife inserted 2 to 3 inches from the edge of the pie will withdraw clean.

Transfer to a cooling rack. When the pie has reached room temperature, prepare the Sweet Cream Topping.

SWEET CREAM TOPPING:

2 cups heavy cream, very cold

3 tablespoons sifted confectioners' sugar

1 teaspoon pure vanilla extract

One 9-inch pie

SWEET CREAM TOPPING

To make the topping, pour the cream into a well-chilled deep bowl. Beat until soft, floppy peaks are formed. Sprinkle with confectioners' sugar, add vanilla, and continue beating until the cream forms firm peaks that hold their shape. Spoon over the chocolate filling, spread to the edge of the pie, and swirl decoratively.

Chill for at least 1 hour before serving.

Mile-High Coconut Cream Pie

¾ cup granulated sugar

¼ cup cornstarch

2 cups light cream, at room temperature

1 cup milk at room temperature

4 extra-large egg yolks, at room temperature, lightly beaten

4 tablespoons (½ stick) unsalted butter, at room temperature

2 teaspoons pure vanilla extract

1 cup sweetened shredded coconut

One fully baked 9-inch pie shell, made from one recipe Flaky Pie Crust (page 21)

A tall meringue caps off this rich coconut pie. The filling is one of those stovetop-cooked puddings made extra creamy by using light cream. The pudding is thickened with cornstarch, which I think works better than flour. The cornstarch binds the liquids and egg yolks into a soft, light-tasting semitranslucent mass.

This coconut pie has become a family favorite ever since the first one was set on the cooling rack. If you're not in the mood to make the meringue topping, serve the pie with a thick covering of sweetened whipped cream (see Sweet Cream Topping, page 97).

Mix the granulated sugar and cornstarch in a large bowl until it resembles a fine talcum powder. Add the light cream in a thin, steady stream, whisking constantly. Beat well. Add the milk in a thin stream, blending thoroughly. Beat in the egg yolks. Pour into a heavy 2-quart saucepan (preferably made of enameled cast iron), set over moderately high heat, and bring to the boil, stirring continuously. When the mixture reaches a hard boil (the bubbles cannot be diminished by stirring) reduce the heat to low, and simmer for 2 minutes, while stirring.

Pour the filling into a medium-size mixing bowl. Beat in the softened butter, a tablespoon at a time, adding the next tablespoon after the first has melted into the pudding. Beat in the vanilla and shredded coconut. Cover the surface of the pudding with a sheet of plastic wrap; let cool for about ½ hour.

To make the meringue topping: Place the egg whites and

10 extra-large egg
  whites, at room
  temperature

¾ cup plus 2 tablespoons
  granulated sugar

¼ teaspoon cream of
  tartar

1 teaspoon pure vanilla
  extract

One 9-inch pie

sugar in the top of a double boiler. Pour 1½ inches of water into the bottom saucepan and bring to a simmer. Set the top pan over the simmering water and warm the whites and sugar, stirring briskly—the whites will warm in about 30 to 35 seconds. Remove saucepan from the simmering water, wipe it dry, and pour the whites into a large, deep mixing bowl. Beat the whites until foamy, add the cream of tartar, and continue beating until soft peaks form. Add the vanilla; beat until firm but moist peaks are formed. The firm peaks should hold their shape in a sharp point, and be smooth and satiny.

Turn the filling into the baked pie shell, and spoon the meringue over the coconut filling, spreading it to the edge of the pastry crust. Make deep, upward swirls in the meringue with the back of a spoon, spatula, or flexible palette knife.

Bake in a preheated 400° oven for about 10 minutes, or until the meringue has browned lightly.

Transfer to a cooling rack. Serve at room temperature.

Banana Cream Pie

¾ cup granulated sugar

¼ cup cornstarch

Pinch of salt

1 cup heavy cream, at room temperature

1 cup light cream, at room temperature

1 cup milk, at room temperature

4 extra-large egg yolks, at room temperature, lightly beaten

4 tablespoons (½ stick) unsalted butter, at room temperature

2 medium-size bananas, firm but ripe

One fully baked 9-inch pie shell, made from one recipe Flaky Pie Crust (page 21)

This pie is a real charmer, with sliced ripe bananas sitting under a vanilla cream filling; it is finished with snowy drifts of whipped cream.

For the best flavor, use bananas that are firm but ripe. Slice them on the diagonal into 1-inch pieces, and have the pudding ready to pour once the last banana has been cut.

————◆◆◆————

Mix the sugar, cornstarch, and salt in a large mixing bowl. Slowly whisk in the heavy cream in a thin, steady stream; whisk in the light cream, a little at a time, then blend in the milk. Whisk in the egg yolks. Pour into a heavy 2-quart saucepan (preferably made of enameled cast iron), set over moderate heat, and bring the contents of the pot to a boil, whisking slowly but constantly. When the mixture reaches a hard boil (the bubbles cannot be diminished by stirring), reduce the heat to low and simmer for 2 minutes, while stirring occasionally.

Pour the filling into a medium-size mixing bowl. Beat in the butter, a tablespoon at a time, adding the next tablespoon after the first has melted into the pudding. Press a sheet of plastic wrap directly over the surface of the pudding. Let cool to warm, about 45 minutes to 1 hour.

Slice the bananas into 1-inch pieces and scatter over the baked pie shell. Pour the filling over the bananas, spreading it evenly to conceal them. Chill for 15 minutes.

SWEET CREAM TOPPING:

1½ cups heavy cream, very cold

2 tablespoons sifted confectioners' sugar

¾ teaspoon pure vanilla extract

_____

One 9-inch pie

SWEET CREAM TOPPING

While the pie is chilling, prepare the Sweet Cream Topping: Pour the cream into a well-chilled deep bowl. Beat until soft peaks are formed. Sprinkle with confectioners' sugar, add vanilla, and continue beating until the cream forms firm peaks that hold their shape. Scoop onto the pie, spread to the edges, and, with the back of a spoon, make deep swirls in the whipped cream.

Chill for at least 1 hour before serving.

Chocolate Silk Pie

1/4 cup light cream

6 ounces bittersweet chocolate, roughly chopped

12 tablespoons (1/4 pound plus 4 tablespoons or 1 1/2 sticks) unsalted butter, at room temperature

4 extra-large eggs, at room temperature, separated

2 teaspoons pure vanilla extract

Pinch of salt

2 tablespoons granulated sugar

1/2 cup heavy cream, very cold

One fully baked 9-inch pie shell, made from one recipe Flaky Pie Crust (page 21)

One 9-inch pie

This is a thick and rich chocolate pie. I like to use a good bittersweet chocolate—one that melts into a dense, creamy mass—with an intense chocolate bouquet (such as Callebaut, Lindt Excellence, or Tobler Tradition).

Vanilla-Scented Whipped Cream (page 131), served alongside wedges of the pie, is a good partner; the light cream balances the dark flavor of the chocolate filling. A steaming pot of freshly brewed coffee or espresso is a perfect companion to thick slices of the pie.

Put the cream, chocolate, and butter in a heavy 1-quart saucepan, set over low heat, and cook slowly until the ingredients have melted. Stir occasionally. Once melted, remove from heat and pour into a large mixing bowl. Beat in the egg yolks, one at a time, then blend in the vanilla and salt. Let the mixture cool to room temperature, about 30 minutes.

Beat egg whites in a deep medium-size mixing bowl until soft peaks are formed, sprinkle with sugar, and continue beating until firm but moist peaks are formed.

Stir a large spoonful of the egg whites into the cooled chocolate mixture, until the whites disappear into the chocolate. Fold through the remaining whites. Beat the heavy cream in a small mixing bowl until firm peaks are formed, then fold into the chocolate mixture.

Pour the filling into the baked pie shell, and smooth the top lightly with a rubber spatula. Refrigerate the pie for 6 hours, or until the filling is firm.

Spicy Sweet Potato Pie

2 cups pureed steamed and peeled sweet potatoes (about 4 small sweet potatoes)

¾ cup granulated sugar blended with 1 teaspoon ground cinnamon, ½ teaspoon ground ginger, and ¼ teaspoon freshly grated nutmeg

3 extra-large eggs, at room temperature

2 tablespoons light molasses

1 cup heavy cream, at room temperature

4 tablespoons unsalted butter, melted and cooled

½ teaspoon pure vanilla extract

One fully baked deep 9-inch pie shell, made from one recipe Flaky Pie Crust (page 21)

One 9-inch pie

This is a smooth sweet potato pie given body and substance by cream, eggs, and spices. A pie such as this is the essence of country itself.

If you like a chunkier pie, don't puree the sweet potatoes—press them with a potato masher to get a lumpy, slightly coarse vegetable.

Oftentimes, I'll buy many pounds of sweet potatoes, steam them, process some into a smooth puree and coarsely mash the rest. Two-cup quantities get turned into sturdy freezer containers, transferred to the freezer, and stockpiled for pie baking throughout the fall and winter.

Spicy Sweet Potato Pie is heavenly served with whipped cream sweetened with liquid brown sugar and flavored with vanilla and a few gratings of nutmeg.

Beat the sweet potatoes and sugar-spice mixture in a large mixing bowl. Add the eggs, one at a time, beating well after each addition. Stir in the molasses, cream, butter, and vanilla.

Pour the filling into the baked pie shell. Bake in a preheated 425° oven for 10 minutes, reduce the oven temperature to 325°, and continue baking for about 35 minutes longer, or until the filling has set completely. A knife inserted 2 inches from the center of the pie will withdraw clean.

Transfer to a cooling rack. Serve barely warm or at room temperature.

Apple Streusel Pie

½ cup granulated sugar

¼ cup light brown sugar, firmly packed

2 tablespoons plus 2 teaspoons cornstarch

½ teaspoon ground cinnamon

¼ teaspoon freshly grated nutmeg

5 cups peeled, cored, and sliced tart cooking apples (about 5 large apples)

One fully baked 9-inch pie shell, made from one recipe Flaky Pie Crust (page 21)

CINNAMON-STREUSEL TOPPING:

¾ cup all-purpose flour

¼ cup granulated sugar

¼ cup light brown sugar, firmly packed

5 tablespoons cold unsalted butter, cut into small chunks

The sweet scent of cinnamon, apples, nutmeg, and butter from this pie perfumes the whole house, making the wait for it seem terribly long.

Use firm, tart cooking apples, such as Granny Smith—they bake tender and succulent while holding their shape. The streusel topping, which serves as a lid, keeps the apples moist and silky as they bake. Streusel is quick to blend together and may conceal almost any sort of fruit filling, be it apple, plum, apricot, blueberry, cherry, raspberry, pear, or peach.

Thoroughly mix together the granulated sugar, light brown sugar, cornstarch, cinnamon, and nutmeg in a large mixing bowl. Add the apples, toss, and let sit for 3 minutes. Heap the apple mixture into the baked pie shell, mounding it slightly toward the center.

To make the topping, blend together the flour, granulated sugar, and light brown sugar in a small mixing bowl. Add the butter and, using two round-bladed knives, cut into the flour mixture until it resembles rough-cut oatmeal. Stir in cinnamon and nutmeg.

Cover completely with the streusel, enclosing the apples and any open spots that peak through. Press down gently without compacting it.

Bake in a preheated 375° oven for about 55 to 60 minutes, or until the apples are tender and the filling bubbles through the streusel, looking like cooked jam.

¼ teaspoon ground
  cinnamon
¼ teaspoon freshly
  grated nutmeg

One 9-inch pie

Transfer to a cooling rack. Serve warm or at room temperature, accompanied by scoops of Double Vanilla Ice Cream (page 130), Vanilla-Scented Whipped Cream (page 131), or Vanilla Pouring Custard (page 129).

Buttermilk Pie

1 cup plus 2 tablespoons
vanilla-flavored
granulated sugar (see
recipe below), or plain
granulated sugar

3 tablespoons all-
purpose flour

3 extra-large eggs, plus 2
extra-large egg yolks,
at room temperature

1 cup buttermilk, at
room temperature

2 teaspoons pure vanilla
extract

8 tablespoons (¼ pound
or 1 stick) unsalted
butter, melted and
cooled

1 tablespoon freshly
squeezed lemon juice

One fully baked 9-inch
pie shell, made from
one recipe Flaky Pie
Crust (page 21)

One 9-inch pie

This pie, firmly built into the American pie-making tradition, is one many cooks turned to when fruit was not available or just too expensive. Buttermilk Pie became the
perfect dessert to make with "goods on hand." It uses simple
dairy staples to make a satisfyingly sweet but pleasantly tart
filling.

Buttermilk pie is characteristically buttery and eggy, and
is a bit richer than a plain custard pie; it is a delight when
made with fresh buttermilk, the kind you can purchase
from a dairy or at a natural food store. I buy buttermilk at
a local Maryland dairy; it boasts big lumps of buttery curds
that float through the rich liquid, and makes one of the best
winter pies I know.

Thoroughly stir together the granulated sugar and flour in
a large mixing bowl. Add the eggs, one at a time, blending
well after each addition. Beat in the egg yolks. Blend in the
buttermilk, vanilla, butter, and lemon juice.

Pour the filling into the baked pie shell. Bake in a preheated 400° oven for 10 minutes, reduce the oven temperature to 325°, and continue baking for about 35 to 40
minutes or until the filling has just set and is slightly puffy.
A knife inserted 2 to 3 inches from the edge of the pie will
withdraw clean.

Transfer to a cooling rack. Serve warm or at room temperature.

Vanilla-Flavored Sugar

To make a batch of vanilla-flavored sugar, measure 6 cups of granulated sugar into a large clean, dry jar or other sturdy storage container. Slit 2 moist vanilla beans down the belly to expose the tiny seeds. Bury the beans in the sugar, cover the jar, and store in a cool pantry or larder. Let "marinate" for at least 1 week, shaking the jar when you think of it, then use the sugar at will. To replenish, add 6 cupfuls more of sugar to the beans and let marinate for a week. The beans will continue to perfume this, and at least one more quantity of sugar. After the third go-round, remove the beans, wipe them clean, cut into 1-inch lengths, and pulverize them to a powder in the food processor or a small, powerful coffee grinder. Use the powder to flavor custards, ice cream, and, of course, pie fillings. About ¼ teaspoon of vanilla powder is equivalent to 2 teaspoons pure vanilla extract.

SPRING
COUNTRY
PIES

SPRING COUNTRY PIES

———————◆◆◆———————

Glazed Strawberry Pie   *112*
Deep-Dish Strawberry-Rhubarb Pie   *113*
Plum-Rhubarb Pie   *114*
Orange-Rhubarb Pie   *115*
Coconut "Candy" Pie   *116*
Shimmery Chocolate Pie   *117*
Mile-High Lemon Cream Pie   *118*
Lemon Slice Pie   *119*
Lemon Pudding Pie   *121*
Lemon-Almond Pie   *122*
Lemon Meringue Pie   *123*
Vanilla Meringue Pie   *124*
Lime Cream Pie   *126*

everal years ago, I was asked to judge a pie-baking contest at an old-fashioned country fair. Since the fair was held during late spring, most of the pies we sampled were filled with strawberry and rhubarb. To my amazement, all the judges were able to work their way through about forty different strawberry and rhubarb pies. All the fillings were crimson or deep pink in color, and the pie crusts were made from a variety of doughs. The best pies were carefully flavored with spices and citrus peel and sweetened with enough sugar to enhance the natural taste of the fruit.

I love a plain unbaked strawberry pie made of whole strawberries folded through a sweetened and thickened, crushed strawberry "jam." Hefty slices of this Glazed Strawberry Pie (page 112) are best served with heaping spoonfuls of whipped cream. I also like the combination of strawberries or plums with sliced rhubarb—sugared, spiced, and baked in a double-crust pie. When I am making a pie of sliced rhubarb and nothing more, the filling is seasoned with orange rind, orange juice, and spices.

Mostly I make these simple pies from berries I have handpicked at a nearby farm. Customers such as myself eagerly work the strawberry patches, exchanging recipes for pies, tarts, and jams while they fill their pails with berries.

Lemon pie, every bit as light and tantalizing as strawberry or rhubarb, is a refreshing sweet to serve in the springtime. The lemon pies in this chapter are sweet, tart, and sometimes creamy. The fillings vary—one is a thickened pudding flavored with lemon juice and grated lemon rind; another is a mixture of paper-thin lemon slices marinated in sugar and combined with beaten eggs; and there is a soft, puffy lemon filling that bakes into a lemon custard bottom and sponge-like top. The filling for the lemon meringue and lemon-almond pies tastes vibrantly sweet and sour. Any of the lemon pies makes an ideal teatime snack with a cool fruit spritzer or pot of hot coffee or tea.

Glazed Strawberry Pie

2 cups (1 pint) whole
  strawberries, hulled

1 tablespoon freshly
  squeezed lemon juice

3 tablespoons cornstarch

1 cup granulated sugar

3 cups (1½ pints) whole
  small strawberries,
  hulled

One fully baked 9-inch
  pie shell, made from
  one recipe Flaky Pie
  Crust (page 21)

One 9-inch pie

A good strawberry pie is a mingling of textures and flavors: the melting crumble of the pie crust, the firm berries, and the clear, cornstarch-thickened berry "jam" that binds it. Two cups of lightly crushed whole berries are cooked with sugar, cornstarch and lemon juice to form a "jam." The remaining whole berries are folded through that mixture (the coating thus creating a glaze) and piled into a baked pastry shell.

Blueberries and blackberries may be substituted for the strawberries, when either fruit abounds.

Dump the 2 cups strawberries into a large bowl, crush lightly with the back of a wooden spoon or with a potato masher, and stir in the lemon juice; set aside.

Thoroughly blend together the cornstarch and sugar until the mixture looks like a fine baby powder. Pour in the crushed strawberries; stir. Turn into a heavy nonreactive saucepan and set over moderate heat. Cook the mixture, stirring, until it comes to a boil and thickens. Remove from the heat, pour into a bowl, and cool to tepid.

When the "jam" is tepid, fold it through the 3 cups whole berries. Pile into the baked pie shell.

Serve at room temperature with Vanilla-Scented Whipped Cream (page 131), if you like.

Deep-Dish Strawberry-Rhubarb Pie

⅓ cup all-purpose flour

1¼ cups granulated sugar

¼ teaspoon ground cinnamon

¼ teaspoon ground allspice

¼ teaspoon ground cloves

Pinch of salt

3 cups small strawberries, hulled

2 cups trimmed and ½-inch sliced rhubarb

2 tablespoons unsalted butter, cut into bits

One recipe Flaky Pie Crust, prepared for a deep-dish pie cover (page 21)

CRUSHED SUGAR GLAZE:

2 tablespoons ice-cold water

12 small sugar cubes, crushed

One 9-inch pie

Nuggets of rhubarb and whole strawberries, sweetened and thickened, turn into a crimson-colored filling when baked. This pie is pleasingly sweet and tart, and very good when accompanied by scoops of Double Vanilla Ice Cream (page 130), which melt into the pie filling.

I love to use a crushed sugar glaze to give the top crust a crunchy exterior. For that, crush small sugar cubes with a rolling pin, mallet, or mortar and pestle, then brush the crust with ice-cold water and sprinkle with the shards of sugar.

Combine the flour, sugar, cinnamon, allspice, cloves, and salt in a large mixing bowl. Add the rhubarb and strawberries, toss well, and let stand for 1 minute.

Spoon the filling into a deep 9-inch pie pan, or any other deep-dish ovenproof vessel (round or oval), mounding the filling slightly toward the center. Dot with butter, cover with the round of dough, seal, and crimp the edges decoratively, as explained on page 27. Refrigerate for 10 minutes.

For the crushed sugar glaze, brush the top of the pie with water and sprinkle with crushed sugar. Cut several steam vents, using a sharp paring knife.

Bake in a preheated 425° oven for 15 minutes. Reduce the oven temperature to 350°, and continue baking for about 35 to 40 minutes longer, or until the pastry is golden.

Transfer to a cooling rack. Serve warm or at room temperature.

Plum-Rhubarb Pie

One recipe Flaky Pie
   Crust for a Double-
   Crust Pie (page 30),
   well chilled

⅓ cup all-purpose flour

1⅓ cups granulated sugar

¼ teaspoon ground
   allspice

¼ teaspoon ground
   cinnamon

¼ teaspoon freshly
   grated nutmeg

Pinch of salt

3 cups sliced and pitted
   ripe red plums

2 cups trimmed and
   ½-inch-sliced rhubarb

1 tablespoon plum syrup
   (page 37)

2 tablespoons unsalted
   butter, cut into bits

MILK AND SUGAR GLAZE:

2 tablespoons cold milk

1 tablespoon granulated
   sugar

One 9-inch pie

The filling for this pie is a sensual mixture of sour-sweet plums and tart rhubarb, balanced by spice-seasoned granulated sugar. I like to moisten the top of the pie with a tablespoon of homemade plum syrup, which brings the flavor of the fruit into bloom. The method for making all sorts of fruit syrups may be found on page 37, at the beginning of the chapter on Summer Country Pies.

---❖❖❖---

Line a 9-inch pie pan with half of the chilled dough following the directions on page 31; refrigerate.

Combine the flour, sugar, allspice, cinnamon, nutmeg, and salt in a large mixing bowl. Add the sliced plums and rhubarb; toss well. Let stand for 2 minutes.

Spoon the filling into the chilled pie shell. Drizzle with plum syrup, dot with butter, cover with the remaining dough, seal, and crimp the edges decoratively, as explained on page 31. Refrigerate for 10 minutes.

For the glaze, brush the top of the pie with milk and sprinkle with sugar. Cut several steam vents, using a sharp paring knife.

Bake in a preheated 425° oven for 15 minutes, reduce the oven temperature to 350°, and continue baking for 35 to 40 minutes longer, or until the top is golden.

Transfer to a cooling rack. Serve barely warm or at room temperature, accompanied by Vanilla Pouring Custard, if you like (page 129).

❖❖❖❖❖❖❖❖❖❖❖❖❖❖❖❖

Orange-Rhubarb Pie

One recipe Flaky Pie
   Crust for a Double-
   Crust Pie (page 30),
   well chilled

⅓ cup all-purpose flour

1½ cups granulated
   sugar

¼ teaspoon ground
   cinnamon

¼ teaspoon ground
   allspice

4 cups trimmed and
   ½-inch sliced rhubarb
   (about 6 long stalks)

1 tablespoon finely
   grated orange rind

2 tablespoons freshly
   squeezed orange juice

2 tablespoons unsalted
   butter, cut into bits

MILK AND SUGAR GLAZE:

2 tablespoons cold milk

1 tablespoon granulated
   sugar

One 9-inch pie

This is a refreshing pie that combines the tart flavor of
rhubarb with the sweet tang of oranges. The ruby-colored
filling is redolent of cinnamon and allspice.

Make this a double-crust pie by covering the filling with a
round of pie dough or enclosing it with an overlapping
pattern of pastry cutouts in the form of hearts, diamonds,
stars, or triangles, as described on page 32. The fanciful
cutout cover looks beautiful and does a perfect job of con-
cealing the filling.

Slices of Orange-Rhubarb Pie are delicious when served
with cups of orange herbal or English Breakfast tea.

Line a 9-inch pie pan with half of the chilled dough following the directions on page 31; refrigerate.

Combine the flour, sugar, cinnamon, and allspice in a
large mixing bowl. Add the sliced rhubarb; toss well. Fold
through the orange rind and lemon juice. Spoon the filling
into the pie shell. Dot with butter.

If you are using the full top crust, cover with remaining
dough, seal, and crimp edges decoratively, as explained on
page 31; if you are using a pastry cutout top, apply cutouts
as explained on page 32. Refrigerate for 10 minutes.

To glaze the crust, brush the top of the pie with milk and
sprinkle with sugar. If you are using a full top crust, cut
several steam vents, using a sharp paring knife.

Bake in a preheated 425° oven for 15 minutes, reduce the
oven temperature to 350°, and continue baking for 40 minutes longer, or until the pastry is golden. Transfer to a
cooling rack. Serve barely warm or at room temperature.

Coconut "Candy" Pie

4 extra-large eggs, plus 1
   extra-large egg yolk,
   at room temperature

1⅓ cups granulated
   sugar

2 teaspoons pure vanilla
   extract

Pinch of salt

8 tablespoons (¼ pound
   or 1 stick) unsalted
   butter, melted and
   cooled

½ teaspoon distilled
   white vinegar

1¼ cups sweetened
   shredded coconut

½ cup chopped pecans

One fully baked 9-inch
   pie shell, made from
   one recipe Flaky Pie
   Crust (page 21)

One 9-inch pie

When the fragile whisked filling for this simple pie bakes, it becomes firm and tastes like a hearty, rich candy bar.

The pie is made from ingredients usually kept on hand in the country pie larder—eggs, sugar, vanilla, butter, coconut, and pecans. It is a light coconut pie, not as rich and filling as coconut cream or any of the custard pies.

Enjoy this pie anytime. Cut in narrow triangular pieces for serving at tea, as the dessert at the close of a Sunday supper, or as a "snacking" pie to nibble on.

———❖❖❖———

Beat the whole eggs and egg yolk in a large mixing bowl. Beat in the sugar, vanilla, and salt. Blend in the melted butter. Stir in the vinegar, coconut, and pecans.

Pour the pie filling into the baked pie shell. Bake in a preheated 350° oven for about 50 minutes, or until set. A knife inserted 2 to 3 inches from the edge will withdraw clean.

Transfer to a cooling rack. Serve at room temperature.

❖❖❖❖❖❖❖❖❖❖❖❖❖❖

Shimmery Chocolate Pie

1⅓ cups granulated sugar

¼ cup sifted unsweetened cocoa powder

1 tablespoon all-purpose flour

Pinch of salt

3 extra-large eggs, plus 1 extra-large egg yolk, at room temperature

¼ cup light cream

2 teaspoons pure vanilla extract

8 tablespoons (¼ pound or 1 stick) unsalted butter, melted and cooled

One fully baked 9-inch pie shell, made from one recipe Flaky Pie Crust (page 21)

One 9-inch pie

This translucent pie has a custard-like quiver to it; it's enriched with cocoa, eggs, and vanilla. Shimmery Chocolate Pie is ideal to serve with a steaming pot of coffee or small cups of espresso, along with a little Vanilla-Scented Whipped Cream on the side (page 131).

Thoroughly blend together the sugar, cocoa, flour, and salt. Beat the eggs and egg yolk together, add to the sugar-cocoa mixture, and beat well. Blend in the cream, vanilla, and butter.

Pour the filling into the baked pie shell. Bake in a preheated 350° oven for 50 minutes or until set. A knife inserted 1 to 2 inches from the center of the pie will emerge clean.

Transfer to a cooling rack. Serve at room temperature with spoonfuls of Vanilla-Scented Whipped Cream, if you like (page 131).

Mile-High Lemon Cream Pie

¼ cup cornstarch

¾ cup granulated sugar

Pinch of salt

2 cups light cream, at room temperature

¾ cup milk, at room temperature

4 extra-large egg yolks, at room temperature, lightly beaten

1 tablespoon finely grated lemon rind

¼ cup freshly squeezed lemon juice

3 tablespoons unsalted butter, softened to room temperature

½ teaspoon pure lemon extract

One fully baked 9-inch pie shell, made from one recipe Flaky Pie Crust (page 21)

This mile-high pie has a flaky crust holding a cooked pudding. The pudding is sparked with lemon and deeply colored by egg yolks. The soft and creamy filling is the base for a dramatic meringue covering made up of 10 egg whites. The soft and thick meringue is a good counterpoint to the eggy richness of the lemon filling.

Thoroughly blend together the cornstarch, sugar, and salt in a large mixing bowl. The mixture should look like a fine talcum powder. Slowly, while whisking, blend in the cream and milk. Whisk in the yolks. Pour into a heavy nonreactive saucepan and set over moderate heat. Stir continuously until the mixture reaches a boil. When the bubbles cannot be stirred down, reduce the heat, and let the pudding simmer for 2 minutes, stirring slowly but continuously.

Remove from the heat, stir in the lemon rind and juice, beat in the butter by tablespoon-size chunks, adding the next only after the first has melted into the pudding, and blend in the lemon extract. Pour into a bowl and press a piece of plastic wrap directly over the surface. Cool the pudding for 25 to 30 minutes, then turn into the baked pie shell.

For the topping, stir together the egg whites and sugar in the top of a double boiler. Set the saucepan containing the whites over a saucepan holding about 1½ inches of barely simmering water. Let the sugar and whites warm over the water for 30 to 35 seconds, stirring constantly. Remove the saucepan, wipe dry, then transfer the whites to a large, deep

10 extra-large egg
  whites, at room
  temperature

¾ cup plus
  2 tablespoons
  granulated sugar

½ teaspoon pure vanilla
  extract

¼ teaspoon cream of
  tartar

One 9-inch pie

mixing bowl. Beat the whites on moderately high speed until frothy, add the vanilla and cream of tartar, and continue beating on high speed until the whites have formed firm but moist peaks.

Pile the meringue on top of the pie filling, spreading it to enclose the filling completely. Peak and swirl the meringue decoratively with a narrow spatula.

Bake in a preheated 400° oven for about 10 minutes, or until the meringue is lightly browned.

Transfer to a cooling rack. Serve at room temperature, preferably no longer than 4 to 5 hours after baking.

❖❖❖❖❖❖❖❖❖❖❖❖❖❖❖

Lemon Slice Pie

One recipe Flaky Pie
  Crust for a Double-
  Crust Pie (page 30),
  well chilled

1 lemon, cut into paper-
  thin slices, seeded

2 lemons, pared to
  remove entire outer
  peel and white pith,
  cut into paper-thin
  slices, seeded

This pie has an intense lemon flavor; whole lemons (both peeled and unpeeled) are thinly sliced as the basis for the filling. The lemon slices are tossed in sugar and left to macerate overnight to lessen the astringency of the lemon peel before combining with the beaten eggs.

Sometimes, if I'm in a playful mood, I'll customize the pastry cover by designing a pastry cutout overlay of whole lemons and lemon leaves. These I apply over the top and use a clear, simple glaze to show off the design. For more casual times, I make a crunchy sugar glaze flavored with lemon to finish off the pie; I rub sugar cubes over the sur-

(continued)

2 cups granulated sugar

4 extra-large eggs, at room temperature

2 tablespoons unsalted butter, cut into bits

CRUSHED LEMON-SUGAR GLAZE:

12 small sugar cubes

1 lemon

2 tablespoons ice-cold water

One 9-inch pie

face of a lemon or two so the essential oils permeate the cubes and turn them a light yellow color. The cubes are crushed and sprinkled over the pie.

Line a 9-inch pie tin with half of the chilled dough, following the directions on page 31; refrigerate.

Combine the sliced lemons and granulated sugar in a large nonreactive mixing bowl. Toss well. Cover the mixture loosely with plastic wrap and let stand at room temperature overnight. Stir the mixture twice.

Beat the eggs in a large mixing bowl. Add the lemon-sugar mixture and stir gently. Pour the filling into the chilled pie shell. Dot with butter, cover with the remaining dough, seal, and crimp the edges decoratively, as explained on page 31. Refrigerate for 10 minutes.

For the lemon-flavored crushed sugar glaze, rub the sugar cubes over the outside of the lemon, letting the cubes absorb the oil. Crush the cubes with a rolling pin.

Brush the top of the pie with water, sprinkle with the crushed sugar, and cut several steam vents using a sharp paring knife.

Bake in a preheated 425° oven for 10 minutes, reduce the oven temperature to 350°, and continue baking for 30 to 35 minutes longer, or until the pastry is golden.

Transfer to a cooling rack. Serve at room temperature.

Lemon
Pudding Pie

4 tablespoons (½ stick)
  unsalted butter,
  softened at room
  temperature

1 cup granulated sugar

3 extra-large egg yolks,
  at room temperature

⅓ cup freshly squeezed
  lemon juice, strained

2 teaspoons finely grated
  lemon rind

3 tablespoons plus 2
  teaspoons all-purpose
  flour

1 cup light cream, at
  room temperature

2 extra-large egg whites,
  at room temperature

Pinch cream of tartar

One fully baked 9-inch
  pie shell, made from
  one recipe Flaky Pie
  Crust (page 21)

One 9-inch pie

The filling for this lemon pie is a light one: butter, sugar, and egg yolks are creamed together and flavored with lemon juice and rind. A bit of flour is added to bind the mixture and cream to smooth it. The resulting batter is lightened considerably with beaten egg whites. Once the filling is poured into a pie shell and baked, something miraculous begins to happen—a soft lemon custard forms a bottom layer while a spongy, cake-like layer rises to the top.

This old-time heirloom-quality recipe is wonderful to make when all you have on hand are a few bakery staples and some juicy lemons.

———❖❖❖———

Cream the butter well in a large mixing bowl. Add ¾ cup granulated sugar in two additions, beating for 1 minute after each portion is added. Blend in the egg yolks, one at a time, beating well after each addition. Beat in the lemon juice and lemon rind; beat in the flour and cream.

Beat the egg whites on moderately high speed in a small, deep bowl until frothy. Add the cream of tartar and continue beating until soft peaks are formed; add the remaining ¼ cup sugar and beat until firm but moist peaks are formed. Stir a small spoonful of the egg whites into the lemon mixture, then fold in the remaining egg whites.

Gently pour the filling into the baked pie shell. Bake in a preheated 400° oven for 10 minutes, reduce the oven temperature to 350°, and continue baking for about 25 minutes longer, or until the top is well-risen and firm to the touch.

Transfer to a cooling rack. Cool completely, then refrigerate for 6 hours before serving.

❖❖❖❖❖❖❖❖❖❖❖❖❖❖❖

Lemon-Almond Pie

1½ cups lemon-scented granulated sugar (at right)

1 tablespoon plus 1 teaspoon cornstarch

1 tablespoon finely grated lemon peel

4 extra-large eggs, plus 1 extra-large egg yolk, at room temperature

¼ cup plus 1 tablespoon freshly squeezed lemon juice, strained

6 tablespoons unsalted butter, melted and cooled

⅓ cup ground blanched almonds

One fully baked 9-inch pie shell, made from one recipe Flaky Pie Crust (page 21)

One 9-inch pie

When the eggs, sugar, butter, lemon juice, and almonds bake in the pie shell, the filling acquires a soft, jelly-like consistency.

To build the lemon flavor, I use lemon-scented granulated sugar in place of plain sugar. Lemon-scented sugar is a delight to have on hand; it adds zest to pie fillings and to fruit syrups used for poaching fruit. The sugar is quick to make: Strip the peel from two lemons. Pour 6 cups granulated sugar into a large, clean jar, add the lemon peel, cover tightly, and shake well. Let stand in a cool pantry for about 1 week, shaking the jar from time to time. After 1 week, discard the lemon peel and add 12 strips of air-dried lemon peel. (To air-dry, leave the strips of peel on a sheet of waxed paper at room temperature for 1 to 2 days.) Cover the jar and store in a cool pantry, where the sugar will keep indefinitely.

———❖❖❖———

Blend sugar and cornstarch in a large mixing bowl. Stir in the lemon peel. Add the eggs and egg yolk, one at a time, beating well after each addition. Stir in the lemon juice, butter, and almonds.

Pour the filling into the baked pie shell. Bake in a preheated 325° oven for about 50 minutes, or until the top is a light golden color and the filling has set; a knife inserted 2 to 3 inches from the edge will withdraw clean.

Transfer to a cooling rack. Serve at room temperature.

Lemon Meringue Pie

1/3 cup cornstarch

1 1/2 cups granulated sugar

Pinch of salt

1 1/2 cups water

4 extra-large egg yolks, at room temperature, lightly beaten

1/4 cup freshly squeezed lemon juice, strained

2 tablespoons finely grated lemon peel

2 tablespoons unsalted butter, cut into small chunks

One fully baked 9-inch pie shell, made from one recipe Flaky Pie Crust (page 21)

MERINGUE TOPPING:

9 extra-large egg whites, at room temperature

3/4 cup granulated sugar

1/4 teaspoon cream of tartar

One 9-inch pie

This is the pie my mother made all through my childhood and teenage years. She adapted the recipe from one printed in *McCall's* magazine many years ago. I still make the filling as my mother did, but I use my pie crust and a more voluptuous meringue. Sometimes I use lemon-scented granulated sugar in place of the plain sugar (page 122).

Thoroughly blend cornstarch, sugar, and salt in large, heavy saucepan. Slowly blend in the water, whisking constantly. Bring to the boil over moderately high heat, stirring. Boil 1 minute. Remove from heat. Stir 1/4 cup of the hot mixture into the yolks, then add the egg yolk mixture to the hot mixture. Bring to the boil, boil 1 minute, and remove from heat. Stir in lemon juice, peel, and butter, a chunk at a time.

Pour the filling into the pie shell.

For the topping, stir the egg whites and sugar in the top of a double boiler. Set the saucepan containing the whites over a saucepan holding about 1 1/2 inches of barely simmering water. Let the sugar and whites warm over the water for 30 to 35 seconds, stirring. Remove the saucepan, wipe dry, then transfer the whites to a large, deep mixing bowl. Beat the whites on moderately high speed until frothy, add the cream of tartar, and continue beating the whites on high speed until firm but moist peaks are formed.

Spread the meringue on top of the pie filling, enclosing it completely. Peak and swirl the meringue decoratively with a narrow spatula. Bake in a preheated 400° oven for about 10 minutes, or until the meringue is lightly browned.

Transfer to a cooling rack. Serve at room temperature.

Vanilla Meringue Pie

¼ cup cornstarch

¾ cup Vanilla-Flavored Sugar (page 107)

¼ teaspoon freshly grated nutmeg

Pinch of salt

2 cups light cream, at room temperature

1 cup heavy cream, at room temperature

4 extra-large egg yolks, at room temperature, lightly beaten

Seed scrapings from the inside of a 3-inch piece of fresh vanilla bean

4 tablespoons unsalted butter, cut into small chunks

2 teaspoons pure vanilla extract

One fully baked 9-inch pie shell, made from one recipe Flaky Pie Crust (page 21)

Cream pies are a joy to make because they rely on only the simplest of things—dairy staples, a heavy pot to make a pudding, and a baked pie shell.

In this pie, the flavor of vanilla comes through in several forms: from liquid extract, vanilla-flavored granulated sugar, and scrapings from a fresh vanilla bean. The creamy, pale yellow filling has specks of vanilla seeds which look and taste appealing.

The vanilla pudding is covered with a meringue, and its soft lightness is a good textural relief from the richness of the pudding.

———◆◆◆———

Thoroughly blend the cornstarch, sugar, nutmeg, and salt in a heavy 2-quart saucepan (preferably made of enameled cast iron). The mixture should look like a fine baby powder. Slowly blend in the light cream, whisking continuously. Blend in the heavy cream. Beat in the egg yolks and seed scrapings from the vanilla bean. Set the saucepan over moderate heat and bring the mixture to a boil, stirring continuously. When the bubbles cannot be stirred down, reduce the heat and let simmer for 2 minutes while stirring.

Remove from the heat. Beat in the chunks of butter, one at a time, adding the next only after the first has melted into the pudding. Beat in the vanilla extract. Pour into a bowl and press a piece of plastic wrap over the surface. Cool the pudding for 30 minutes, then turn it into the baked pie shell.

For the topping, stir together the egg whites and sugar in

9 extra-large egg whites,
   at room temperature
¾ cup granulated sugar
¼ teaspoon cream of
   tartar

One 9-inch pie

the top of a double boiler. Set the saucepan containing the whites over a saucepan holding about 1½ inches of barely simmering water. Let the sugar and whites warm over the water for 30 to 35 seconds, stirring continuously. Remove the saucepan, wipe dry, then transfer the whites to a large, deep mixing bowl. Beat the whites on moderately high speed until frothy, add the cream of tartar, and continue beating on high speed until the whites have formed firm but moist peaks.

Pile the meringue on top of the pie filling, spreading it to enclose the filling completely. Peak and swirl the meringue decoratively with a narrow spatula.

Bake in a preheated 400° oven for 10 minutes, or until the meringue is lightly browned.

Transfer to a cooling rack. Serve at room temperature, preferably no longer than 4 to 5 hours after baking.

Lime Cream Pie

5 extra-large egg yolks,
   at room temperature

1 14-ounce can
   sweetened condensed
   milk

7 tablespoons fresh or
   bottled Key lime juice

One fully baked 9-inch
   pie shell, made from
   one recipe Flaky Pie
   Crust (page 21)

WHIPPED CREAM TOPPING:

2 cups cold heavy cream

¼ cup sifted
   confectioners' sugar

4 to 5 tablespoons lightly
   toasted sweetened
   shredded coconut

One 9-inch pie

The filling for this pie uses the tart juice from Key limes, which, along with sweetened condensed milk and plenty of egg yolks, makes a delicious sweet-sour filling. When baked and cooled completely, the lime custard layer is covered with a thick mantle of lightly sweetened whipped cream and sprinkled with toasted coconut.

The penetrating flavor of the limes makes this a sprightly pie to serve anytime, but I love to have it on hand for dessert in early spring to recharge the winter-weary taste buds.

Beat the egg yolks in a medium-size mixing bowl until combined. Blend in the milk and lime juice. Pour the filling into the baked pie shell. Bake in a preheated 350° oven for 15 to 20 minutes, or until it is set, and a knife inserted 2 to 3 inches from the edge of the pie will withdraw clean.

Transfer to a cooling rack. Cool to room temperature.

For the whipped cream topping, beat the heavy cream in a deep, chilled bowl until soft peaks are formed. Sprinkle with confectioners' sugar, and continue beating. Beat until it holds its shape in firm peaks.

Spoon the cream over the pie filling, spreading it to cover the filling entirely. With the back of a spoon, make deep swirls in the cream. Chill in the refrigerator for at least 3 hours. Just before serving, sprinkle with toasted coconut.

Substitution Note: Bottled Key lime juice is an excellent substitute for fresh limes if they are not available. I particularly like Nellie and Joe's Key West Lime Juice, available in 16-ounce bottles.

SWEET AND CREAMY PIE COMPANIONS

Vanilla Pouring Custard, Double Vanilla Ice Cream, and Vanilla-Scented Whipped Cream are lovely accompaniments to a slice of country pie. These may be scooped, puddled, or spooned over and about a helping of pie.

I love the way the pouring custard runs into the juice of a fruit pie filling, faintly tinting the juice a soft pastel color, and the way a puff of sweetened whipped cream plays against the richness of all the nut, chocolate, and mincemeat pies. Pie served à la mode is delicious, too. Vanilla ice cream enhances all of the fruit pies, rich pies such as my Coconut-Walnut-Chocolate-Chip "Candy" Pie (page 86) and the streusel-topped pies—Apple Streusel Pie (page 104), Cinnamon-Pear Pie with Walnut Streusel (page 69), and Peach Streusel Pie (page 38), among them.

Vanilla Pouring Custard

1 small vanilla bean

1¼ cups light cream

3 extra-large egg yolks, at room temperature

1¼ teaspoon arrowroot

3 tablespoons granulated sugar

1 teaspoon pure vanilla extract

Enough pouring custard to accompany one country pie

This is a smooth, cream-enriched custard sauce, lightly thickened with egg yolks and flavored with vanilla.

Serve a pitcher with any of the fruit or mincemeat-filled country pies. I love the way the soft, lightly scented sauce mingles with the juices when poured over each slice.

Slit the vanilla bean down the center (without cutting through the whole bean) to expose the tiny seeds. Pour the cream into a small, heavy saucepan; add the vanilla bean. Scald over moderately high heat, remove from heat, and set aside.

Beat the egg yolks in a large mixing bowl for 1 minute. Add the arrowroot and sugar, and continue beating until thick and light.

Remove the vanilla bean from the cream. Add the cream slowly to the egg yolk mixture, whisking all the while. Pour into a heavy saucepan, set over low heat, and cook slowly, stirring continuously with a wooden spoon, until the mixture thickens. The custard is ready when it lightly coats the back of a wooden spoon. Off the heat, stir in the vanilla.

Strain through a fine-meshed sieve into a bowl. If you are not serving the custard warm, sprinkle the top with a fine haze of superfine sugar to keep a skin from forming.

Use the custard warm, at room temperature, or chilled, ladled from a small, deep bowl or poured from a decorative pitcher.

Double Vanilla Ice Cream

1 plump, fat vanilla bean

2 cups light cream

¾ cup granulated sugar

5 extra-large egg yolks, at room temperature

Pinch of salt

1 tablespoon pure vanilla extract

1¾ cups heavy cream, cold

½ cup milk, cold

Enough vanilla ice cream to accompany two country pies

Rich and cooling, this vanilla ice cream may bring back to life the nostalgic ritual of hand-cranking ice cream. It's one of those simple pleasures that ought to be revived. Have a favorite country pie on the cooling rack, then gather everyone to churn the following creamy mixture into a frozen delight.

This is a good ice cream for pies, made of sweet cream, plenty of egg yolks, sugar, and vanilla. (I use the tiny seeds scraped out from the inside of the vanilla bean, the scraped-out bean itself, and pure vanilla extract to flavor the ice cream.)

Double Vanilla Ice Cream is a fine plate mate for a slice of any oven-fresh fruit pie—apple, pear, mincemeat, rhubarb, peach, plum, nectarine, blueberry, blackberry, red raspberry, black raspberry, or strawberry.

———❖❖❖———

Slit the vanilla bean down the belly to expose the tiny seeds using a sharp paring knife. With the tip of a small spoon, scrape the seeds into a heavy, medium-size saucepan. Add the scraped-out bean and the light cream. Scald over moderately high heat. Remove from heat, add the salt, and set aside.

Put the sugar and egg yolks in a large mixing bowl; beat well until slightly thickened. Strain the cream through a fine-meshed sieve. Add to the egg yolk and sugar mixture slowly, a few tablespoons at a time, whisking well. Discard the vanilla bean.

Pour into a medium-size heavy saucepan. Cook slowly, stirring continuously, over low heat until slightly thickened, and the custard lightly coats the back of a wooden spoon. Remove from the heat, stir in the vanilla, and let cool to room temperature.

Stir the heavy cream and milk into the custard, pour into a storage container, cover, and refrigerate for about 6 hours, overnight, or until well chilled.

Freeze in a hand-cranked or electric ice cream maker, according to the manufacturer's directions.

❖❖❖❖❖❖❖❖❖❖❖❖❖❖❖❖❖

Vanilla-Scented Whipped Cream

1½ cups very cold heavy cream

3 tablespoons sifted confectioners' sugar

1 teaspoon pure vanilla extract

Enough whipped cream to accompany one country pie

This cloud-light dessert sauce is designed to add creaminess to a warm slab of pie. A puff of lightly sweetened whipped cream with a bit of vanilla is a welcome accompaniment to down-home country pies. The sauce marries beautifully with those pies built on apples, pears, peaches, nectarines, plums, and rhubarb; all of autumn's squash and summer's berries; and almost any pie containing chocolate or nuts, pecans in particular.

———❖❖❖———

Pour the cream into a well-chilled, deep bowl. Whip until it begins to mound very lightly. Sprinkle with confectioners' sugar; stir. Stir in the vanilla extract. Continue beating until gentle, floppy peaks are formed. The whipped cream should hold its shape softly in a spoon.

Turn into a bowl and serve dollops alongside a helping of pie.

THE COUNTRY PIE SWAP

J ust like a cookie swap, a country pie swap is an informal dessert party where everyone can bring a favorite pie, exchange recipes and gossip, and dip into luscious wedges of freshly baked pie.

Organize a pie swap as a neighborhood party, holiday gathering, or Sunday afternoon tea-and-coffee klatch. Encourage guests to bring their pies nestled in carrying baskets or in deep serving platters. A large bread board is a good base for a pie, as is a round pressed-glass, narrow-lipped cake plate lined with doilies. A Shaker pie carrier, made of interconnected wooden slats, looks beautiful holding a pie. Line it with a crisp, colorful tea towel or antique piece of lace before you set in the pie.

The gathering of pies looks pretty—and tempting—assembled on a table or sideboard, with a selection of iced or hot tea and coffee set up nearby. Offer bowls of whipped cream or ice cream on the side if you like.

If you are hosting the swap, make sure no two pies are alike, and try to arrange for a variety of fillings. Gently persuade people to bring a pie they are known for. And remind each pie-baker to bring copies of his or her own pie recipe (including both crust and filling) to hand out to the other guests.

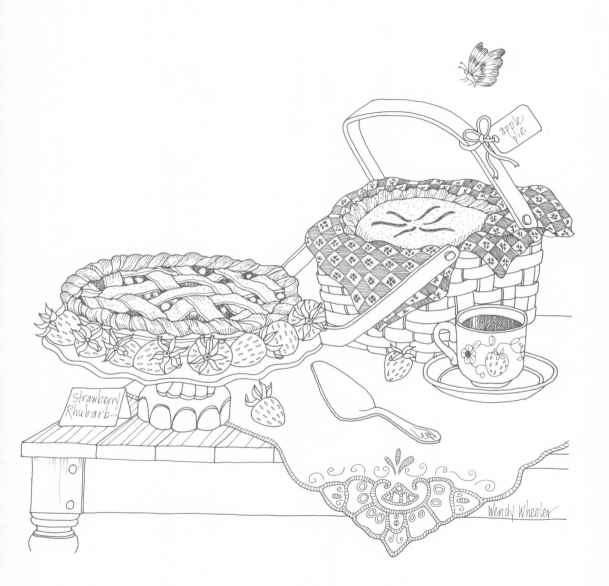

apple
pie

Strawberry
Rhubarb

Wendy Wheeler

Country Pies That Use Fresh Fruits and Vegetables

———— ❖❖❖ ————

Peach Streusel Pie   38
Deep-Dish Gingered Peach Pie   40
Double-Crust Blueberry-Peach Pie   42
Deep-Dish Blueberry Pie   44
Spiced Red Plum Pie   45
Prune Plum Pie   46
Deep-Dish Walnut-Rum-Plum Pie   46
Double-Crust Nectarine Spice Pie   48
Sour Cherry Pie   50
Glazed Yellow Cherry Pie   51
Deep-Dish Blackberry Pie   52
Apple-Raspberry Pie   53
Red Raspberry Pie   54
Fresh Apricot Pie   55
Late Season Green Tomato Pie   56
Double-Crust Apple Pie   62
Apple-Ginger Mincemeat Pie   63
Apple-Pear Pie with Apple Cider Syrup   66
Pear Mincemeat Pie   68
Cinnamon-Pear Pie with Walnut Streusel   69

Spiced Pear-Currant Pie   71
Cranberry-Walnut Mincemeat Pie   72
Pumpkin Custard Pie   76
Pumpkin Crunch Pie   78
Fresh Sugar Pumpkin Pie   80
Apricot-Yam Pie   81
Orange-Butternut Squash Pie   82
Brandied Golden Acorn Squash Pie   84
Banana Cream Pie   100
Spicy Sweet Potato Pie   103
Apple Streusel Pie   104
Glazed Strawberry Pie   112
Deep-Dish Strawberry-Rhubarb Pie   113
Plum-Rhubarb Pie   114
Orange-Rhubarb Pie   115
Mile-High Lemon Cream Pie   118
Lemon Slice Pie   119
Lemon Pudding Pie   121
Lemon-Almond Pie   122
Lemon Meringue Pie   123
Lime Cream Pie   126

Country Pies That Use "Goods on Hand" (Basic Dairy and Pantry Staples)

———————— ❖❖❖ ————————

Golden Pecan Pie   74
Bourbon Pecan Pie   75
Coconut-Walnut-Chocolate-Chip "Candy" Pie   86
Brown Sugar Pie   87
Vanilla Custard Pie   92
Coconut Custard Pie   93
Maple Cream Pie   94
Maple-Walnut Pie   95
Old-Fashioned Chocolate Fudge Pie   96
Mile-High Coconut Cream Pie   98
Chocolate Silk Pie   102
Buttermilk Pie   106
Coconut "Candy" Pie   116
Shimmery Chocolate Pie   117
Vanilla Meringue Pie   124

Index

———◈◈◈———

A

Acorn squash, golden
  pie, brandied, 84
  puree, 85
Almond-lemon pie, 122
Apple cider syrup, 65
   apple-pear pie with, 66
Apple pie
  double-crust, 62
  ginger mincemeat, 63
  pear-, with apple cider syrup, 66
  raspberry-, 53
  streusel, 104
Apricot pie
  fresh, 55
  yam-, 81

B

Banana cream pie, 100
Blackberry pie, deep-dish, 52
Blueberry pie
  deep-dish, 44
  peach-, double-crust, 42
Bourbon pecan pie, 75
Brandied golden acorn squash pie,
  84
Brown sugar pie, 87
Buttermilk pie, 106
Butternut squash
  pie, orange-, 82
  puree, 83

C

"Candy" pie
  coconut, 116
  walnut chocolate-chip, 86
Cherry pie
  sour, 50
  yellow, glazed, 51
Chocolate pie
  fudge, old-fashioned, 96
  shimmery, 117
  silk, 102
Chocolate-chip-coconut-walnut "candy"
  pie, 86
Cinnamon-pear pie with walnut streusel,
  69
Coconut
  "candy" pie, 116
   walnut chocolate-chip, 86
  cream pie, mile-high, 98
  custard pie, 93
Cranberry
  preserve, 73
  -walnut mincemeat pie, 72
Cream, whipped, vanilla-scented, 131
Cream pie
  banana, 100
  coconut, mile-high, 98
  lemon, mile-high, 118
  lime, 126
  maple, 94
Currant-pear pie, spiced, 71
Custard
  pie
   buttermilk, 106

Custard pie *(cont.)*
    coconut, 93
    pumpkin, 76
    vanilla, 92
   pouring, vanilla, 129
Cutout pastry top, 32–33

D

Dried fruit and spice mincemeat, 64

E

Edges for pie crusts, 27–29

F

Fruit
    dried, and spice mincemeat, 64
    syrups, to make, 37–38
Fudge pie, chocolate, old-fashioned,
    96

G

Ginger(ed)
   -apple mincemeat pie, 63
   peach pie, deep-dish, 40
Golden pecan pie, 74
Green tomato pie, late season, 56

I

Ice cream, double vanilla, 130
Ingredients, 15–16

L

Lattice cover for a double-crust pie, 33
Lemon
   -almond pie, 122
   cream pie, mile-high, 118
   meringue pie, 123
   pudding pie, 121
   slice pie, 119
Lime cream pie, 126

M

Maple
   cream pie, 94
   -walnut pie, 95
Meringue pie
   lemon, 123
   vanilla, 124
Mile-high coconut cream pie, 98
Mile-high lemon cream pie, 118
Mincemeat
   dried fruit and spice, 64
   pie
     apple-ginger, 63
     cranberry-walnut, 72
     pear, 68

N

Nectarine spice pie, double-crust, 48

O

Orange-butternut squash pie, 82
Orange-rhubarb pie, 115

P

Pans, pie, 18–19
Pastry cutouts
    to add to the top of a deep-dish or
        double-crust pie, 33–34
    to fashion a pie cover of, 32–33
Peach pie
    blueberry-, double-crust, 42
    gingered, deep-dish, 40
    with streusel topping, 38
Pear pie
    apple-, with apple cider syrup, 66
    cinnamon-, with walnut streusel, 69
    currant-, spiced, 71
    mincemeat, 68
Pecan pie
    bourbon, 75
    golden, 74
Pie crust, flaky, 20–34
    about, 20
    for a single-crust pie, 20–26
        about, 21
    to completely prebake a pie shell, 24

Pie crust, flaky (cont.)
    to cover a deep-dish pie with a
        round of pie dough, 23–24
    to freeze pie crust dough, 31
    to freeze a pie shell, 25
    to line a rimmed pie pan, 22–23
    to make the dough by hand, 21
    to make the dough in a food
        processor, 22
    to roll out the pie dough, 22
    variations, 25–26
    to waterproof the pie shell, 24–25
   for double-crust pie, 30–34
    to add extra pastry cutouts, 33–34
    cutout pastry top, 32–33
    food processor method, 30–31
    hand method, 30
    lattice cover for, 33
    to line a rimmed pie pan for, 31–32
    to roll out the pie dough, 31
    variations, 34
   edges for, 27–29
Plum pie
    red, spiced, 45
    rhubarb-, 114
    walnut-rum-, deep-dish, 46
Prebaking pie shells, 24
Preserve, cranberry, 73
Pudding pie lemon, 121
Pumpkin
    pie
        crunch, 78
        custard, 76
        sugar pumpkin, fresh, 80

Pumpkin *(cont.)*
    puree
        fresh, 77
        sugar pumpkin, fresh, 80

R

Raspberry pie
    apple-, 53
    red, 54
Red plum pie, spiced, 45
Rhubarb pie
    orange-, 115
    plum-, 114
    strawberry-, deep-dish, 113
Rum
    -plum-walnut pie, deep-dish, 46
    syrup, 47

S

Sour cherry pie, 50
Squash
    acorn
        pie, brandied, 84
        puree, 85
    butternut
        pie, orange-, 82
        puree, 83
Strawberry pie
    glazed, 112
    rhubarb-, deep-dish, 113

Streusel topping
    apple pie with, 104
    peach pie with, 38
    walnut, cinnamon-pear pie with, 69
Sugar
    flavored, 15–16
        vanilla-, 107
    pie, brown, 87
Sugar pumpkin pie, fresh, 80
Sweet potato pie, spicy, 103
Syrup
    apple cider, 65
        apple-pear pie with, 66
    to make, 37–38
    rum, 47

V

Vanilla
    custard pie, 92
    -flavored sugar, 107
    ice cream, double, 130
    meringue pie, 124
    pouring custard, 129
    -scented whipped cream, 131

W

Walnut
    coconut chocolate-chip "candy" pie,
        86
    -cranberry mincemeat pie, 72

Walnut *(cont.)*
   -maple pie, 95
   -rum-plum pie, deep-dish, 46
   streusel, cinnamon-pear pie with,
     69
Waterproofing pie shells, 24–25

Y

Yam
   pie, apricot-, 81
   puree, 81